The
A to Z
of
DARTMOOR TORS

Terry Bound

"Tors are scattered all over the moors. Many are landmarks which can be seen for miles. They have a magnetism I can't resist… The smaller, less shapely tors which don't get in the guidebooks have lured me to some fine wilderness country. These little outcrops maintain an exclusive, rather remote air of privacy."

BRIAN CARTER

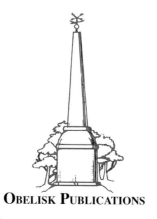

OBELISK PUBLICATIONS

ALSO BY THE AUTHOR

The Great Walks of Dartmoor
Walks in the Chagford Countryside

OTHER DARTMOOR TITLES FROM OBELISK PUBLICATIONS

The Great Little Dartmoor Book, *Chips Barber*
The Great Little Chagford Book, *Chips Barber*
Dark & Dastardly Dartmoor, *Sally & Chips Barber*
Dartmoor of Yesteryear, *Chips Barber*
Ten Family Walks on Dartmoor, *Sally & Chips Barber*
Six Short Pub Walks on Dartmoor, *Sally & Chips Barber*
Colourful Dartmoor, *Chips Barber*
Cranmere Pool – The First Dartmoor Letterbox, *Chips Barber*
The Teign Valley of Yesteryear, Parts I and II *Chips Barber*
Princetown of Yesteryear Parts I and II, *Chips Barber*
Widecombe – A Visitor's Guide, *Chips Barber*
Railways on and around Dartmoor, *Chips Barber*
The Story of Dartmoor Prison, *Chips Barber*
Lydford and Brent Tor, *Chips Barber*
Along The Tavy, *Chips Barber*
Around and About Tavistock, *Chips Barber*
Around and About Roborough Down, *Chips Barber*
Around and About Lustleigh, *Chips Barber*
The Dartmoor Quiz Book, *Chips Barber*
The Templer Way, *Derek Beavis*
Walks in the Shadow of Dartmoor, *Denis McCallum*
Walks in Tamar and Tavy Country, *Denis McCallum*
A Dartmoor Boyhood, *David Lee*
Dartmoor Letterboxing–A Guide for Beginners, *Kevin Weall*
*We have many other Devon titles. For a current list please send an SAE to
Obelisk Publications, 2 Church Hill, Pinhoe, Exeter, EX4 9ER.
Or visit our website at www.ObeliskPublications.com*

This book is dedicated to Alison and Graham.

ACKNOWLEDGEMENTS: All photographs are by Chips Barber including cover photographs of Doe Tor and Brat Tor. All pictures are positioned within the text to which they refer. Many sincere thanks are due to Martin and Dennis for their companionship, and many other friends and fellow members of the Long Distance Walkers Association and of the Dartmoor Walking Group, formerly the V.T. Walking Club. Thanks also to John Weir at the National Park for checking the manuscript so carefully – hopefully any mistakes are now minimal! All views and opinions expressed are entirely my own.

All positions of tors, rocks, obstacles, objects of any kind and details of access are as accurate as is possible but do not in any way constitute permission to reach them. If in any doubt, please contact the Dartmoor National Park Authority.

*First published in 1991 (0 946651 43 4)
Revised edition (1 899073 27 2) published in 1995
This edition published in 2011 by
Obelisk Publications, 2 Church Hill, Pinhoe, Exeter, Devon
Printed in Great Britain by Short Run Press Ltd, Exeter*

> **TOR:**
> "Hill, rocky peak, esp. on Dartmoor, O.E. perhaps derived fr. Gaelic 'torr' = hill"
> *Concise Oxford Dictionary*
> "Hill, rocky height. O.E. torr. Latin: turris = tower, or perhaps Celtic"
> *Chamber's 20th Century Dictionary*
> "fr. Celtic, 'twr' = tower"
> William Crossing: *Guide to Dartmoor*
> "A hill, more usually a hill crowned with rock and recently used for the crowning mass itself"
> R. Hansford Worth: *Dartmoor*
> "Any high hill on top of which ground is grouped ... a collection of huge granite Boulders"
> "BA": *A Gentleman's Walking Tour of Dartmoor*

These are just a few definitions of the word TOR from the mouths of experts. But when is a tor not a tor? Why do some rock-crowned hills not bear the word tor in their name? Well I class a tor as *any* outcrop of rock or rocks – and my aim in this book is to present a detailed catalogue of all Dartmoor tors, whatever their position.

The list is based mainly (but certainly not wholly) upon the Ordnance Survey's placings and spellings, along with alternative names from other Dartmoor authors. In *Walking the Dartmoor Railroads*, Eric Hemery says, "Names of many features as they appear on current OS maps… are mistranscriptions. The authentic spellings are used." If that is the case, one wonders why Samuel Rowe, Richard Hansford Worth, Sabine Baring-Gould and William Crossing consistently used them?

Also included are tors referred to by other authors, e.g. Snappers Tor, referred to by Crossing but not on the 1:25 000 maps. A few of the names that appear on the maps incorporate tor but without any sign of outcrops; they are misleading and sites such as Higher and Lower Tors near Bel Tor would probably refer to the former small wood which once grew there. Similarly, Brousentor near Baggator has no rocky stack in the immediate vicinity. I have omitted these 'bogus' intruders from the list. Several, at least 100, tors are not named on the 1:25 000 OS maps, so the grid references are particularly relevant.

Having said that, there must be scores of rock piles that have no names, or at least not having had a name ever put into print. Therefore, the list must end somewhere, and I have only included 'tors' and the more substantial or prominent rocks.

Rough Tor, East Mill Tor and Yes Tor

I have been fortunate to have companions who are just as keen as I am to explore the moor, in all its moods, and the places where the usual visitor rarely seeks. Thanks are also due in this revised version to John Chambers and Bernard Lane who have helped me in the researching and locating of newly found tors. Thus, I have visited every unenclosed tor in the list, bar two, plus a few (unintentionally) that are privately owned, and nearly all the off-moor rocks. I trust therefore, that the list is as comprehensive as humanly possible...

EXPLANATION OF CATALOGUE

Each tor is listed alphabetically with its **Name** as it appears on the OS 1:25 000 Leisure Map – otherwise, the source of the name is added [in brackets]; followed by **Area** of moor between name and grid reference; then **Grid Reference;** next to which is the **Height** above sea level, in metres; finishing with any relevant **Details** which are indicated by letters thus:

F: in wood or forest
H: army hut or observation post on or near tor
K: on the 1240 perambulation ('k' for knights)
M: the tor consists of more than one outcrop or pile
N: not on access land
O: outside the Dartmoor National Park
P: flagpole on or near tor
Q: quarry on tor
R: on ridge or summit of hill
T: OS triangulation pillar (trig. point) on or near
W: tor used as part of wall
X: 'off-moor' tors

This information is then followed by **Other Spellings** or forms with **Source**. Letters are used to indicate the following sources of alternative names:

D: 1086 Domesday Book
B: 1240 perambulation account as reported by Spence Bate
J: 1823 J. P. Jones
BA: 1864 *A Gentleman's Walking Tour of Dartmoor* by 'BA' (nom-de-plume)
JC: 1892 J. Chudleigh: *An Exploration of Dartmoor's Antiquities*
SR: various publications by Samuel Rowe including 1609 and 1896 perambulation accounts
C: 1912 William Crossing: *Guide to Dartmoor*
RW: 1953 (pub) Richard Hansford Worth: *Dartmoor*
EH: 1980-86 various publications by Eric Hemery

Further Information includes: other tors seen from this point, with distances and bearings based on the 32 points of the mariners' compass; rivers, streams and valleys where appropriate; a brief description of the tor if worthy of note; plus access from suitable parking places – how to get there!

I have used the metric system throughout as most walkers will have use of a map of some description and, if they are Ordnance Survey maps, it is easy to work out distances, i.e. one square on the map is a kilometre in either direction: (one mile = 1.6 km approx.; 5 miles = 8 km, and so on). Height is also in metres (8 m = 25 ft; 16 m = 50 ft; 32 m = 100 ft approx).

The A to Z of DARTMOOR TORS

AISH TOR   Dart   702715   +283
Mel Tor 1.3 km NW; Leigh Tor 1 km W; Bench Tor W. Access from Poundsgate on Dartmeet road.
The village is 1 km N and has a shop and pub, the Tavistock Arms, where the Devil called one evening and instead of ordering his usual black-and-tan, indulged in something more expensive and paid the landlord in leaves.
Dr Blackall's Drive makes a semi-circle around the hill on which Aish Tor lies. The doctor and his friends were keen carriage riders and the chance arose for him to have a route aligned above the Dart Gorge. The track can be followed from Bel Tor Corner from where it zigzags towards Mel Tor; it affords spectacular views across the tree-covered slopes of the Dart. The drive crosses the Poundsgate–Dartmeet road near the top of the hill above Spitchwick where Dr Blackall owned the manor house. There is no tor on this hill though.

ANSWELL ROCK see Ausewell Rocks

ARCH TOR   Postbridge   633782   c.412
Two or three large cuboid rocks.
Longaford Tor 2 km W; Crockern Tor 3 km SW; Littaford Tor 2 km WSW; Bellever Tor 2 km SSE; Cherrybrook 500 m W; Powdermills leat flows on the E-S-W to the mills (see Longaford Tor).
Arch Tor is visible from the B3212 south-west of Postbridge, but appears as if someone has dropped stones on a hill; it is hardly worth the name tor.

ARMS TOR   Lyd   541863   457   M R
Brat Tor 700 m S; Gt Links Tor 1.25 km ENE; Sourton Tors 3.5 km N; Hare Tor 2.25 km SSE; R. Lyd 600 m W; Smallacombe Brook 1.25 km NE.
Access is from the Dartmoor Inn on the A386 near Lydford. Turn east up the track to the large car park, then via High Down follow the wall on the north of the grass to cross the Lyd by a footbridge, bearing slightly left as you go uphill to the piles.

ASHBURY TOR [c]   Okehampton   604940   309   R
Belstone Tor 2.25 km SSE; Yes Tor 4.5 km SSW; Cleave Tor E over Okement; Moor Brook S in steep wooded valley; E. Okement 300 m E.
A footpath runs to the tor from the west and another leads north towards the Okehampton by-pass (A30) branching to the town over the road or down to Fatherford Viaduct to the NNE, 600 m away. Few rocks are in sight from the north, but they appear as a cliff from the south and east. The E. Okement runs north through West Cleave, which is one of William Crossing's 'Gems'.

AUSEWELL ROCKS   Buckland   731716   250   F N
Answell Rock [SR] Hazel Rocks [JC] + [SR] Hazel Tor [C] + [SR]
Eden Phillpotts also used the name Hazel Tor in the novel *Orphan Dinah*. *Buckland Beacon 1.5 km N.*
It is 750 m from Ashburton to the Buckland-in-the-Moor road. The rocks are in **private** woodland. The Dart is to the west; these woods form part of Dart Chase, the former hunting grounds of the local lords.

BAG TOR   Haytor   762757   +349   R
Bagathora [D]
Rippon Tor 1.75 km W; Saddle Tor 1.5 km NW; Haytor N; R. Sig to the W and S; R. Lemon E.
Access to the tor is by the gate at GR 761760, via the lower car park below Haytor (the one with the toilets) and above the remains of Bag Tor Mine to the east (left) as you walk SSW for about 1.5 km. One of Crossing's 'Gems', Bagtor Mill is on the road to the south-east of the tor on the R. Lemon.

BAGGA TOR **Willsworthy** **548806** **372** **N R**
Bog Tor [sr]
White Tor 2 km SSW; Lynch Tor 1.75 km E; Baggator Brook 400 m N; Youlden Brook 400 m S.
As tors go this one is relatively easy to climb for a better view from the top. I don't recommend that every tor should be 'conquered' but some are easier than others and Bagga Tor is one such. It is just north of the Lich Way, 50 m or so, and is reached by driving to the moorgate at Wapsworthy (GR 547805).

BAIRDOWN TOR see Beardown Tors

BARE DOWN TOR see Beardown Tors

BARN HILL ROCKS [eh] **Tavistock** **535746** **330**
Overlooking the 'Blacksmith's Shop' on the eastern slope of Barn Hill. The smith cared for the horses used in transporting the granite from Staple and Pew Tor quarries.

BEACON ROCKS see Ugborough Beacon

BEARDOWN TORS **W. Dart** **602774** **512** **H M P R**
Bairdown Tor [jc] + [sr] **Bare Down Tor** [sr]
Crow Tor 1.5 km NNE; Longaford Tor 1.25 km SE, with Higher White to the left and Littaford to the right; Gt Mis Tor 4 km S of W; Lydford Tor 1 km NNW. Other rocks are within view of the tor but the directions of many of them vary depending from which of the four large piles you view them. West Dart 600 m E of the SE outcrop.
The southerly piles look over Bellever Forest, which was planted in 1919. Devonport Leat is taken from the Dart to the east; it runs through the forest, contouring the slope around to the west, where it meets the R. Cowsic before continuing its 40 km journey across the moor to Burrator. Access to the tors is from Two Bridges by way of a public footpath. It is marked on the OS Leisure map, and can be traced through a gate and stile on the west of the road bridge, up the west bank of the R. Cowsic to Beardown Farm Bridge. Then through the farm itself, following the signposts, up to the leat to turn east (right) through the wood. You emerge and cross the leat at the yellow dot and aim for the gate in the last wall before the open moor. The tor lies ahead of you to the north-west. Wistman's Wood, also noted under Longaford Tor, is a 'Gem', too.

BEARYONDER TOR see White Tor, Lower

BEE TOR **Moretonhampstead** **708844** **317** **R**
Begatora [d]
Not on common land. Visible from the B3212 road from Lettaford Cross (GR 710841) N to Furze Park, behind which the tor stands. It can also be seen if you travel NE from Postbridge, coming downhill after the cattle grid at Leapra Cross (where the Mariners' Way passes across the B3212).

BEE TOR, LITTLE **W. Dart** **616767** **466** **M R**
Bee Tor [sr]
Longbetor on Donn's map is shown where Littaford Tor is.
Some maps show Littaford Tors; I believe that the pile 20 m S of Littaford, a separate outcrop, is in fact, Little Bee. Longaford Tor 1 km N; Crockern Tor 1.5 km S. Other tors are as from Littaford, as is also the walk to these rocks from Two Bridges.

BEGATORA see Bee Tor

BEL TOR **Dart** **697730** **354** **R N**
Bell Tor [bg]
Mel Tor 500 m SW; Sharp Tor 1 km W; one cliff-like formation to the east is less than 100 m away; R. Dart S; W. Webburn NE.
This tor is not accessible to the public.

BELL TOR **Widecombe** **730778** **400** **M R**
Haytor 2.5 km ESE; Bonehill Rocks 400 m SSE; Chinkwell Tor 250 m NNW.
See Sharp Tor, Widecombe.

Bell Tor is the higher of the major outcrops on the ascent from the road below Bonehill Rocks.

BELLEVER TOR   Postbridge   644764   441   M R T
Bellaford Tor [JC]

Sittaford Tor 7 km N; Birch Tor 6.5 km NNE; Hameldown Tor 7 km NE; Haytor 11 km E; Rippon Tor 10 km ESE; Yar Tor 4 km SE; North Hessary Tor 7 km WSW; Gt Mis Tor 8 km W; Beardown Tor 4 km WNW; Higher White Tor 3.25 km NW; Cherrybrook W; East Dart E, beyond which is Laughter Tor, 1 km SE.

An excellent example of an avenue tor, like West Mill Tor, Hound Tor and Pil Tor.

Three or four main piles dominate the area and this is one of them. For many kilometres around it is easy to recognise, rising above forestry land. This was established between the wars and to some people's horror, covered some antiquities to the north but, as a concession, the Forestry Commission has allowed a wood-free wedge on the side of Lakehead Hill, stretching north from the tor.

Before the 1939–1945 war, horse-racing and events for the local population took place annually in May, when Bellever Fair Day was celebrated. A similar show took place near Huccaby Tor.

From the main car park at Postbridge, cross the road and walk through the forest on the wide track that leads due south. Signposts will take you to the open moor when you will see Bellever Tor straight in front of you.

BELSTONE TOR   Belstone   614921   479   K M R

Cosdon Beacon 2.25 km ESE; Steeperton Tor 3 km E of S; Oke Tor 2 km S; East Mill Tor 2 km SSW; Yes Tor 3.75 km SW.

The many stacks cover a distance from north–south of over 500 m, with the most southerly pile, Higher Tor standing over a vast expanse of grass and isolated trees, a different outlook from the ridge where all of both east and west slopes are masses of clitter and large boulders. The R. Taw runs northwards 600 m off to the E while the E. Okement 900 m to the W, passes under Cullever Steps, on the parish boundary between Okehampton and Belstone.

You will notice a ruined wall, which climbs up to the middle range from one side and down the other in almost a straight line. This is referred to as Irishman's Wall, the story being that an Irish gentleman decided to take up the moorland custom of owning what could be enclosed by a permanent wall. Whether he worked on his own or not, we are not told, but villagers and a band of Okehampton men proceeded to Belstone Tors, spread themselves out along the wall, and "threw it down", as Crossing says. Quite a lot is still intact, however.

Belstone Tor(s) are reached by parking before the village. Walk through Belstone, bearing right at the green and left at 'Belmonte' to the moorgate. Then walk 1 km S to the first of the tors high above (it seems). It is worth keeping to the ridge to visit all the high-spots of the range.

BENCH TOR — Dart — 691716 — 323 — M R

Benjie Tor [SR] + [EH] also the local pronunciation

Mel Tor 600 m N; Buckland Beacon 4 km ENE; Aish Tor 1 km E; Luckey Tor 700 km WNW; Laughter Tor 5 km NW with Bellever Tor behind it; Sharp Tor 1.25 km NNW; R. Dart flows from NW-NE-SE. Venford or Wennaford Brook runs into the Dart on the west, issuing from Venford reservoir.

A line of outcrops on a north-south bearing stand above the valley in a spectacular fashion, but because the Dart wends its way in great loops, the tor is not seen to great advantage. From Mel Tor and Hockinstone Tor (ENE below), Bench Tor appears in its best light. It is an easy walk to Bench Tor from the car park to the east of Venford Reservoir. Go 800 m due north. You may see RD over an H on stones over a metre high around the man-made lake. These stand for Richard Dawson, Holne, the landowner from whom Paignton Urban District Council bought the rights to build the dam, thus enabling a better water supply to that town.

BERRA TOR — Tavistock — 479690 — c.130 — N O X

R. Tavy 600 m W.

Set against the hillside, the tor is surrounded by woodland and faces south. It is a cliff-like formation roughly 6 m high. It is accessible only across farmland from the lane which runs north from the hamlet of Coppicetown. There is no public right of way.

BERRA TOR see Burra Tor

BIG ROCK [EH] — Tavy — 527799 — F W

East of Horndon at the south end of Creason Wood roughly half way along the Hill Bridge Leat. A public footpath runs alongside it from Hill Bridge to the north-east to a track near Horndon.

BILLY'S TOR [EH] — Princetown — 569745 — 450

King's Tor 1.5 km SW; Gt Staple 3 km NW; Gt Mis Tor 2.5 km NNW.

Millions of years ago, there was a tower of rocks on the site; time, nature and the elements have reduced it to a jumble of boulders. The views are excellent, especially on a clear day! From Four Winds walk 1 km SE.

BIRCH TOR — Warren House — 688816 — 487 — M R

Shapley Tor 1.25 km ENE; Hameldown Tor 2 km SE; Bellever Tor c. 7 km SW; East Bovey Head 1 km NE; the springs of the West Webburn SE; North Wallabrook 1 km W; Redwater SW.

About 100 m separate the extreme rock-piles of Birch Tor, situated in a line in a vaguely N–S arrangement. The whole area to the south of the rocks is a mass of gullies, pits, ruins and the occasional metal implement associated with mining. The Golden Dagger Mine was one of the success stories of the mines on Dartmoor; 220 tons of tin ore was extracted in thirty years around the turn of the century. It did not close down until the outbreak of the Second World War. Birch Tor and Vitifer Mines were forerunners in the production of tin and the leat that brought water to the area can be traced south-westwards to beyond Grey Wethers nearly 8 km away. The site of another warren also lies to the south of the tor. Headland Warren supplied the miners with a regular amount of rabbit meat. The farm of the same name is still occupied. Around Birch Tor, and extending to the B3212 and the road from Widecombe to Challacombe Cross, are many erect stones bearing WB, for Warren Bounds. Dave Brewer has accounted for at least sixteen of these markers. One of them, Bennet's Cross, stands near the road next to the parking space from where you can walk to Birch Tor. Be careful, however, as some of the gullies mentioned are in a direct line with your objective and I cannot be held responsible for broken limbs! Soussons Wood, 1 km S, was established in 1946 and is the newest of the conifer plantations on the moor. A footpath runs from Bennet's Cross through the forest; once in the woods, the going can be sticky.

BLACK ROCK   Lyd   531855   c.300

On the right bank of the R. Lyd, with Brat Tor above. An iron plaque bears a poem commemorating Capt. Hunter, who died in France at the end of the First World War (see Brat Tor).

BLACK TOR   Avon   681635   320   M R

Eastern Whittabarrow 2 km NNW; Shipley Tor 500 m SE; Sharp (Wacka) Tor 2 km SW; Three Barrows (Tor) 3 km WSW; R. Avon E flowing S from Avon Dam Reservoir, 1.5 km to the north.

A more modern construction, the dam was started in 1954, and has a catchment area of much of the south-east moor. It's a shame that an arrangement could not have been made to plant trees around the water, as at Fernworthy, or is the cost beyond reach? Even a mixed woodland would be better than a bare hillside although many walkers abhor acres and acres of coniferous forest. There are five main stacks to the tor, the highest on level ground to the west. The grass here is short and in golf course condition so is easy to walk on. The 'invisible' Zeal Tor is 1 km NW.

After parking at Shipley Bridge, take the road northwards (South West Water vehicles only) for 1 km. On the way, at the junction of the lane to the treatment works and and the road to the dam, you pass the Hunters' Stone. On it is carved the names of each of the Masters of the South Devon Hunt. Further on, on the left, are the ruins of Brentmoor House, at one time the home of William Petre, who owned much of the moor from the Avon to the Erme. (Petre's Pits and Petre's Cross, on W. Whittabarrow are named after him.) Go past these remains; when the wall slopes up to the left, follow it and after a short, sharp effort, reach the top and the rocks.

BLACK TOR [SR]   Erme   655584   c.330

W. Beacon 800 m S, on the row of stones; Ugborough Beacon 1.25 km NE.

Samuel Rowe's mention of a tor here (1898) seemed at first surprising, but when I explored the area in search of it, I found no obvious pile as such, but there is a small stack 10 m to the east of the line of boundary-markers, halfway up the first rise going north from Black Pool, roughly 250 m S of the summit of Butterdown Hill.

BLACK TOR   Meavy   573718   363   M

Hart Tor 1 km WNW; Cramber Tor 1 km SE; Leeden Tor 1 km W; R. Meavy E-S.

The R. Meavy flowing over Black Tor falls, is a beauty spot frequented by many. Some visitors even manage to find and recognise the two blowing houses on either side of the water. The one on the left bank has a well-preserved chimney with XIII on the lintel.

A hundred metres or so below the huts is the aqueduct taking the Devonport Leat over the river. The rusty pipe which is in evidence in the valley takes off water from the Meavy to supplement the flow of the leat. Further down, 60 per cent of the water in the leat drops into Burrator Reservoir and the rest enters Dousland Reservoir which provides that village and Yelverton. Clearly seen from the B3212, Black Tor is approached from the small parking spot 200 m N.

BLACK TOR   W. Okement   567895   488   M

High Willhays 1.5 km E; Lints Tor 2.25 km SE; Stenga Tor 1.5 km S; Shelstone Tor 1 km WNW.

The W. Okement flows below from SE to NW, running past Blackator Copse, one of the three native woodland areas on the moor. The trees here are taller than those in Wistman's Wood. Fine views from the top are had to the north-east over mid-Devon, but the deep valley is one of my favourite scenes. Starting at Meldon Dam, keep to the east of the water for 2 km; after passing the stone bridge on the right next to a shed, keep south-east for another 1.5 km, avoiding marshy ground by aiming for the tor above and at an angle slightly away from the river.

BLACKADON TOR   Dart/Buckland   712734   270

Honeybag Tor and Chinkwell Tor 5 km NNE; Rippon Tor 4 km NE; Buckland Beacon 2.25 km E; Bel Tor (almost hidden) 2 km WSW; Yar Tor 3.5 km WNW; Rowden Tor 3 km NNW; West Webburn N and unites with East Webburn N to run E towards the R. Dart to the S.

Lizwell Meet, where the two Webburns flow together, is one of Crossing's 'Gems'. A low grassy mound, the tor doesn't rise above 3 m, its tallest wall being on the east. Many gorse bushes and a number of hawthorns make this quite a delightful scene and, combined with the views of wooded valleys, it should be more popular than it appears to be as evidenced by the lack of erosion in the vicinity. Leusdon Church, 200 m W, is the scene of a legend (but true) of Tom French and is found on page 103 of 'Gems'. Access is easy – parking is not. A stop on the green at Leusdon may be the only answer as the lane leading from the hamlet to the Dart Valley will not cater for tor visitors. However, you won't mind the walk; just past Leusdon Manor, a hotel on the right of the road, turn left between two walls and in 100 m, at a Nature Reserve sign, go left uphill for 200 m to the tor.

BLACKALDER TOR   Lee Moor   568616   234   O

Whitehill Tor 700 m ESE.

Erroneously called "Blackadder Tor" because of the proliferation of rowans in the vicinity! The tor is dominated by the two white piles behind it but one is, at the time of writing, being reclothed with vegetation; a somewhat compromising policy by English China Clays but one to applaud after the necessary evil of removing kaolin from the region. The works began in 1830 soon after William Cookworthy realised the primary use of the material, and now eighty per cent of the clay is exported; its usage ranges from giving magazines their gloss to numerous additives in pharmacological preparations.

BLACKATON TOR   Widecombe   694785   381

Hameldon Beacon 1.5 km E; Riddon Ridge 4 km SW.

Access is through a gate from the road leading northwards from Widecombe, bear left around scrubby area and gently climb to the summit.

BLACKATOR [C GILL]   East Dart   665750   c.300   E W

Yar Tor 1.5 km SE; E Dart River 300 m E.

In *Dartmoor: a New Study*, which Gill edited, the map on page 158 shows an outcrop east of Brimpts Newtake which can be safely assumed to be the tor as Blackator Rocks are shown to be on the actual bank of the Dart 100 m from the outcrop. From Huccaby Cottage, go northwards on the path keeping to the edge of the plantation. At the wall, go north-east and where the wood ends, carry on to find the tor which is 1.5 km from the road.

BLACKEY TOR [RW]   Princetown   612737   360
Colden Tor [C]

Blackabrook 500 m N; Cholake, which is only 1 km long, 600 m E.

A large number of 3 m high piles, facing north over the former brook, are found amid examples of kists (stone chests). The "Crock of Gold" shown on the OS map is on the other side of the fence, 800 m away to the south-east. Access is best from the Tor Royal to Swincombe track, from which you take the stile nearest to the Crock of Gold and walk northwest to the rocks.

BLACKINGSTONE ROCK   Moreton   787856   +355   X
Blackeystone Rock [SR]
Blackstone Rock [J, who adds that "it is not
connected with the devil"]
Blackystone Rock [JC]

An example of a stack being formed by lamellar bedding of granite. Steps lead up to the top of the 25 m high pile. The rock is named on a signpost at Cossick Cross on the B3212 between Doccombe and Moretonhampstead. A short drive to a stile and gate takes you to within 100 m of the rock.

BOG TOR see Baggator

BONEHILL ROCKS   **Widecombe**   **731774**   **393**

A large tor-like formation with many overhangs; one of a line of rocky masses from Honeybag Tor in the north to Whitabarrow to the south of the ridge.

BOTTOR ROCK   **Bovey Tracey**   **827805**   **240**   **W X**

The farthest east of the tors close to and halfway along the bridleway south-west of Hennock. A visit to this tor could be included in a walk to Shaptor Rock and Gladstone Rock.

BOULTERS TOR   **Peter Tavy**   **525781**   **336**   **R W**

White Tor 2 km ENE; Great Mis Tor 4 km ESE; Great Staple Tor 2.5 km SE; Cox Tor 2 km SSE; Collybrook S.

The main pile is on the eastern part of Smeardown with the other stacks positioned about 70 m apart going westwards. The tor(s) lie to the north of the peat-workers path to Walkham Head from the villages of the valley; an unnamed stack is on the immediate right of the track just before Boulters Tor on the left. An easy route to follow but involving a steady climb: go up the road east from Peter Tavy church for 1.25 km, park if you've come by car, and continue going eastwards. A footpath sign pointing north leads to Cudlipptown beyond the tor.

BOWERMAN'S NOSE   **Manaton**   **742804**   **c.400**

Southcott Rocks [EH]

Hayne Down Tor NW 100 m E; Easdon Tor 2.5 km NNW; Cripdon Down Tors 0.5 km W; Honeybag Tor 2 km SW. See Hayne Down Tors.

Situated on Hayne Down, the "nose" is a 7 m-high pillar assuming the shape of a … nose (with a bit of imagination).

BRANSCOMBE'S LOAF   **Sourton**   **553891**   **+530**

Brandscombe's Loaf [SR]

Bronescombe's Loaf [EH]

Sourton Tors are 1.25 km NW, High Willhays 3 km E.

A single mass of lamellar bedding; a legend is connected with the rock, where a Bishop of Exeter, chased by the Devil, dropped his bread at this spot and a lump of cheese a little to the west.

BRAT TOR   **Lyd**   **539855**   **452**   **R**

Bra Tor [C] + [SR] + [JC]

Brai Tor [EH]

Broad Tor [SR]

Arms Tor 700 m N; Great Links Tor 1.5 km NE; Hare Tor 1.75 km SE; Doe Tor 800 m SSE; Brentor 8.5 km SW; R. Lyd 900 m W; Doe Tor Brook 500 m S.

Seen and recognised from the Okehampton to Tavistock road (A386) with the 4 m high cross on its summit. The only cross on the moor to be of more than one section, it was erected to commemorate the Golden Jubilee of Queen Victoria in 1887. A mass of clitter falls away to the west and south, but to the less steep side only a few boulders lie strewn around. To the west, on the west bank of the Lyd, Black Rock is seen. It is not shown on the OS map, but it is worth a look if only to read the poem on the metal plate affixed to the cliff. Written by Captain Nigel Hunter who lived locally, it evokes the spot graphically; on his last visit to this place, he wrote:

Are we not like this moorland stream	*Wandering thus for many a mile*
Springing none knows where from	*Twisting and turning away for a while*
Tinkling, bubbling, flashing gleam	*Then all of a sudden 'tis over the fall*
Back at the sun; ere long	*And the dark, still pool is the end of all*
Gloomy and dull, under a cloud	*Is it? I thought, as I turned away,*
Then rushing onward again	*And I turned again to the silent moor.*
Dashing at rocks with anger loud	*Is it? I said and my heart said, "Nay",*
Roaring and foaming in vain?	*As I gazed at the cross on "Widgery Tor".*

F. J. Widgery was a Dartmoor artist who enabled the cross to be set up on Brat Tor.

BRENTOR   Lyd   470805   355   R

Sometimes spelt in two words. *Brat Tor 8.5 km NE; Great Links Tor 10 km NE; Hare Tor 8 km ENE; Lynch Tor 9 km E; Great Mis Tor 5 km ESE; Cox Tor 4 km SE in front of Great Staple Tor.*
This is the most westerly of the Dartmoor Tors; as you can tell by the distances to the other visible heights, it is also out on a limb. After a look at the history displayed on a board at the foot of the hill, a short, sharp climb will take you to a building at the top; the legend associated with Brentor and St Michael's Church has been well documented in several other publications. However, few people realise that the summit lies on a ley-line running across southern England in a general south-westerly direction. It passes through Crediton Parish Church, Burrow Mump near Bridgwater, Glastonbury Tor and other prominent heights which are in a direct line from the church at Bury St Edmunds in Suffolk and St Michael's Mount, Cornwall. Is it a pure coincidence, or are these sites really sources of hidden power?

BRIMHILL TOR   Peter Tavy   519794   c.210   N (edge)F
The furthest north-east of the set of tors between Horndon Bridge and Peter Tavy, Brimhill Tor overlooks the Tavy on the south-east and a small valley which is south-east of Bennet's Reservoir (see Kents Tor). It is on private land but can be seen from the lane going north-east from Cudlipptown.

BROAD DOWN   East Dart   635805   c.470   W
Sittaford Tor 2.5 km N; Stannon Tor ENE; Hartland Tor SE.
A low rock, covered in grass and unseen from a distance because it is lower than the walls around it.

BROAD TOR see Brat Tor

BROADOWN TOR [CRISPIN GILL]
On page 49 of *Dartmoor: a New Study*, a line reads: "a [badger's] sett may be found far from woodland, such as those at Lur Tor, near Broadown and Bellever Tors".
Neither of the first two tors are shown on the OS maps and unless they are now obscured by conifer plantations, I have not noticed any other tors in the region apart from Bellever and Laughter Tors. Lur Tor may be an older version of Laughter, but the connection is somewhat vague and the tors may therefore be local names given to minute outcrops.

BRONESCOMBE'S LOAF see Branscombe's Loaf

BUCKLAND BEACON   Buckland   735731   +380   R
Famous for the stones bearing the Ten Commandments, which took six weeks to complete in 1928. Less well-known, there is another carved rock which refers to the setting up of a beacon, one of a chain of fires lit to commemorate the silver Jubilee of King George V and Queen Mary.

BUCKTOR   Tavy/Walkham   480701   c.60   O
On the north bank of the Walkham, Bucktor does not stand proud of the surrounding land but lies flat against the hillside, hiding itself among the numerous gorse bushes. At times, the colour of the rock matches the grey of neighbouring trees and shrubs. At around 10 m long ('high' may give the wrong impression) the tor can be reached from Grenofen (on the A386 between Yelverton and Tavistock) by way of a footpath following the river for over a kilometre before it bears west. The rock is above you before you meet the houses near the river bank. This footpath is found by taking the lane going south-west initially from close to the Halfway Inn, turning left in 250 m and taking the waymarked path just before the bridge. The OS map shows "Buckator" at this site.

BULLATON ROCK	Lustleigh	796822	270	X
BURRA TOR	Burrator	553679	c.220	F Q

Berra Tor [EH]

The quarry was begun when the dam at the reservoir was being built and, like Claig Tor, is close enough to the road to be easily accessible. From the east side of the dam, go south through the gate, or over the stile, and gradually climb to the tor, about 100 m from the entrance to the wood. Were it not for the trees, the tor would be most prominent: you can't see the rocks for the wood!

BUTTERN HILL	Throwleigh	652887	413	M R

Buttern Tor [C]
Buttern Rocks [EH]

Kes Tor 2.75 km SSE; Rival Tor 1 km SW; Watern Tor 3 km SW; Steeperton Tor 3.5 km W; Cosdon Beacon 3.25 km NNW; Wallabrook and North Teign confluence 1.5 km S; Ruelake 1.25 km W

A few small piles crown the hill but they are less obvious than many similar tors. Two routes from the top of the rise may be taken: from Berrydown (GR 663879), where a few cars can be parked, go south-west between walls, then north-west uphill for a kilometre to Buttern Tor; or, from Buttern Lawn (GR 659896), follow the track roughly south-west for just over 1 km to the tor.

CADWORTHY TOR	Plym	542641	210	R

Oxon Tor

From Shaugh Bridge, cross the R. Plym and follow the worn path up through the woods to the top. Turn right towards the rocky summit of Dewerstone to the tor. If you turn half-left at the top of the path to the flat rocks, you should be able to find references to local poets, such as N.T. Carrington.

CALLISHAM TOR	Yelverton	538664	c.220	E

Sharpitor 4.5 km NNE; Sheepstor 3.5 km NE; Shell Top 6.5 km ESE; Cox Tor c. 10 km W of N; Brentor 15 km NNW; Gt Staple Tor 9 km N.

On a footpath from Meavy, the tor is nothing but a jumble of boulders which fall from a 1.5 m high stack for 25 m downhill. These boulders are on the "wrong" side of a wall. In the 1990s a wire fence was erected along the wall making access impracticable.

CALVESLAKE TOR	Plym	608676	400	M

On the open moor, facing the R. Plym to the north and west. Calveslake itself is a small trickle of a stream to the north-east. Harter Tors are on the opposite bank 800 m W.

The tor comprises several small and closely packed piles and is on the same large area of land supervised by the National Trust. Approach the tor from Burcombe Lane, the road from Sheepstor running east, and stay on the track which goes ENE for 2 km until the ruins of Wheal Ruth are reached. Walk SSE to Higher Harter Tor, then to Lower Harter Tor and then to Calveslake Tor, crossing the river.

CASTOR see Kes Tor

CATHANGER ROCK		684749	c.400	R

Corndon Tor 700m S; Yar Tor 800m SW; Hameldown Ridge 3.5km NE; R Webburn 1.5km E.

An isolated rock but accompanied by a few trees. It overlooks Sherwell (pronounced 'Sherril') in the valley and is close to what may well be an ancient but little used path from Shallowford and the Webburn valley to the east, to Sherwell and the East Dart valley to the west.

CATOR	Postbridge	671776	c.320	N

Large boulders set against a grassy bank. Not on access land, but the tor can be seen from the left-hand gateway near the bridge on the Widecombe to Poundsgate road.

CAWSAND see Cosdon Beacon

CHAT TOR	Rattlebrook	555853	541	R

Clatter Tor [SR]

Green Tor 1.25 km NNE; Fur Tor 4 km SE; Hare Tor 1.25 km SSW; Sharp Tor 700 m SW; Great Links Tor 1.25 km NNW; Rattlebrook 500 m E; Deadlake 800 m S; Doe Tor Brook 1 km W.

Almost a Branscombe's Loaf part 2 – a single mass of bedded granite (see Watern Tor and Little Links Tor), it shows up against the skyline from along the ridge from the track to Bleak House in the north, to the top of the bank above Deadlake. Best reached from High Down, take the path between Arms Tor and Brat Tor; after 2 km, in the valley of Doe Tor Brook, bear SSE for1 km.

CHINKWELL TOR   Widecombe   729781   458   M R
Clinkwell Tor [JC]
Honeybag Tor 400 m N; Hound Tor 1.75 km NE; Haytor 3 km ESE; Bell Tor 250 m SSE; Pil Tor 2.25 km E of S.
Two cairns crown the top of the rise among short rocky outcrops but the whole range commands a grand view all around and can itself be seen from many other high-spots in the east of the moor. Chinkwell can be reached from the spot on the road between Bonehill Rocks and Bell Tor by continuing uphill to the summit.

CLAIG TOR [EH]   Burrator   549677   c.230
Sharpitor 3 km NNE; Sheepstor 1.5 km ENE; Gutter Tor 3km ESE; Burra Tor is across the valley of the R. Meavy with the reservoir to the left of it.
Only mentioned in *Walking the Dartmoor Waterways*, p. 80, many people pass by this cliff-like tor without noticing it. Standing by the road from Dousland to Burrator Reservoir, it is about 750 m from the junction south of the village. It has been partially quarried and the parking spot is found at the base of the cliff. A climb up the side of the rocks is the obvious route but an easier way can be found by making a gradual ascent from Burrator Dam up to the track of the former Princetown railway which passes close to the tor.

CLARET TOR [C] + [EH]   Ivybridge   666587   330   M
The exact position of the tor is uncertain; a large rock, 2.5 m long by 1.5 m high is seen on the north-west slope of Eastern Beacon, but on the south-west slope, away from Eastern Beacon is a more conspicuous outcrop. The tor to which the writers refer is probably the larger outcrop of Creber's Rocks, 200 m up from Main Head (the stream flowing southwards in the valley).

CLATTER TOR see Chat Tor

CLAY TOR [C]   Walkham   570781   430   M
Claytor Moor [EH]
Crossing in fact says that "no tor exists", but the area, north of the river and east of Deadlake, is given to assorted rocks and boulders. The biggest pile is 500 m E of Deadlock and 100 m N of the Walkham with the tumuli of Greena Ball to the SSW. Claytor Moor is south-west of Cocks Hill. From Princetown, go via Great Mis Tor, north to the Deadlake confluence then turn east to the rocks. They are on the promontory facing Greena Ball.

CLEAVE TOR [C]   Belstone   609939   300   M R
From Belstone Green, go past the old Vicarage to the commons on the west edge of the parish. The tor is on the brow of the hill; it's another of those tors which do not appear as a stack until you are standing on top of it, because the top of the tor is level with the terrain. There is a very steep, rocky face similar to Ashbury Tor (q.v.) from which Cleave Tor is seen across E. Okement valley.

CLICK TOR [c]   **Deancombe**   **578685**   **c.300**   **N**
Cuckoo Rock 500 m ENE; Combeshead Tor 900 m ENE; Down Tor 800 m N.
In his *Guide to Dartmoor*, William Crossing describes the location of Click Tor, from which I have deduced that the present-day name is Outcombe Rocks. There are no other formations in the immediate vicinity; the rocks are on the eastern edge of the woodland (mixed) over a kilometre from the head of Burrator Reservoir. In 1992 the forest was cleared and the tor became visible from the opposite bank of the Deancombe. It was also more easily accessible for the walker; other outcrops were identified across the valley.

CLINKWELL TOR see Chinkwell Tor

COCKS TOR see Cox Tor

COCKS TOR, LITTLE [EH]   **Tavistock**   **527762**   **c.380**
Cox Tor summit not visible but 300 m N of E; Sharp Tor 1 km NNW; Pew Tor 2.5 km SSE. Large rocks with a few trees growing among them. From Pork Hill car park 1 km NNW, or after seeing Cox Tor.

COLDEN TOR see Blackey Tor

COLLARD TOR   **Lee Moor**   **558621**   **c.250**   **R**
Hawks Tor 600 m NW; Torrybrook 1.75 km SE.
Extensive china clay works to the north and east. Whatever desecration of this part of the moor has taken place – many decry the wholesale damage done to the surface and the millions of cubic metres of rock removed – there are moves afoot to include this region as part of the National Park. It is not only the more aesthetic areas which are part of the moor's natural beauty, but Lee Moor is part of Dartmoor's heritage, if not its history, as well as being an integral part of the lives of many residents in the south-west of Dartmoor. English China Clays, the proprietors, have gone to great lengths to re-establish the surface by landscaping and planting and, given time, the scenery will be pleasing to the eye although appearing somewhat artificial. The tor is on the footpath which leads from Wotter to Hawks Tor going NW, or you can start from a small parking place just west of Moorlands Hotel and go 500 m E past many concrete ruins.

COMBE TOR, GREAT   **Peter Tavy**   **523775**   **260**   **R**
Sharp Tor 300 m SE; Little Combe Tor 300 m NW; Boulters Tor 650 m NNE; White Tor 2.5 km NE; Gt Mis Tor 4 km S of E; Roos Tor 2.25 km ESE; Collybrook N; R. Tavy 2 km W.
In appearance a messy tor: piles of rock forming one mass, they tilt towards the valley. If the rock was granite, not slate, there would be a tidier look to the place! Great Combe Tor is on the Quarryman's Path which leads from Peter Tavy to Merrivale; it is approached from the village along the bank of the Collybrook following the footpath signs over the water then 500 m further.

COMBE TOR, LITTLE   **Peter Tavy**   **521777**   **c.250**
Gt Combe Tor 300 m SE.
Surrounded by oak trees and covered with moss, it's a very pleasant little tor. The large slabs are tilted to lie parallel to the slope and are therefore dangerous to climb onto, unlike most of the tors. Although the views are restricted, the whole valley is in itself attractive, especially in the Spring, and Crossing numbers this valley as a 'Gem'. Access to this tor is gained by using the same footpath as to Gt Combe Tor, but keep on the north side of the brook for 300 m past the bridge. The tor is only 75 m from the water and north of the path.

COMBESHEAD TOR   **Deancombe**   **588687**   **371**   **M R**
Down Tor 1 km NW; Butter Tor 2 km SSW; Eylesbarrow 1 km W; Narrator Brook S and E.
A feature of this tor is the amount of walls in all directions. Those to the south are more substantial and covered in vegetation; to the west and north, much of the material has been knocked over to gain access. However, it is clear that the number of enclosures now unused is due to the building of the lake at Burrator. Several of what we would now call smallholdings, as well as larger farms, were deserted before the turn of the century, as the planners needed the supply of water flowing into the reservoir to be as uncontaminated as possible: untreated manure may easily have found its way into the running water. The water board simply obtained a compulsory purchase order.

Deancombe to the south of the tor is another of William Crossing's 'Gems'! From the car park at the eastern end of Burrator Reservoir, Norsworthy Bridge, take the stony track which leads south (the road bears south-west) and soon passes more abandoned farms. Keep to the riverside as much as possible but beware of a few boggy patches after wet spells. After the end of the woodland on the right of you, go on for 1.5 km until you reach a grassy, treeless patch and, at a row of stepping stones, turn north-eastwards up a worn path. Above a grassy bank you will find a cave set into another wall – this is a potato cave, once used to store root-crops when not needed, where it was dark, cool and not too damp. Continue on the same bearing to the top of the hill and reach the tor.

COMBESTONE TOR — Dart — 670718 — 356 — M R
Combeston Tor [SR]
Cumsdon Tor [JC] + [SR]
Cumston Tor [C] + [EH]

Sharp Tor 2 km NE; Rippon Tor 8.5 km ENE; Buckland Beacon 6.5 km ENE; Huccaby Tor 2.5 km NW; Longaford Tor 8 km NW; Bellever Tor 5 km NNW; Laughter Tor 4 km NNW; West Dart W and N; Double Dart (i.e. West and East Dart combined NE and E).
Access is no problem; a car park has been made for people to walk on a level and even surface to the tor no more than 10 m away! Wheal Emma Leat and Holne Leats nearly surround the rocks. They provide a water supply to mines above Buckfastleigh and to Michelcombe, respectively. Refer to Eric Hemery's *Walking the Dartmoor Waterways* for in-depth descriptions.

CONIES DOWN TOR — Cowsic — 589791 — 520 — M R
Devil's Tor 1 km ENE; Lydford Tor 1.5 km SE; N. Hessary Tor 5 km SSW; Gt Mis Tor 3.5 km SW; Cowsic R. 300 m E; Conies Down Water 600 m S.
The tor lies north of the route of the Lich Way, which crosses the Cowsic at Travellers' Ford, shown on OS maps as Broad Hole. The easiest way to the rocks is from Holming Beam (GR 592764). Walk north, keeping on the same contour to avoid springs, to cross Conies Down Water after 2 km. The tor is seen ahead before you drop down to the stream; it is beyond the clitter met while climbing the slope.

COOMBE TOR — Chagford — 686871 — 25 — F N R W
Meldon Hill 1.5 km SE; Gidleigh Tor 1.5 km NW in woods; Kes Tor 2.25 km WSW.
In private grounds.
From Chagford, take the road towards Kestor (Rock). Just past the junctions after 1 km, Waye is on the right. The drive goes past Way Barton and to the south of Coombe Tor in 250 m.

CORNDON TOR — Dart — 687742 — c.400 — R
Curnen Tor [JC]
Yar Tor 1 km W; Bel Tor 1.5 km SE; Sharp Tor 1.5 km S; W. Webburn valley E; Rowbrook to the right of Sharp Tor (SW).
The summit of the hill has a small tor and two large cairns, four if you count others on the ridge 300 m N. The major rocks which constitute Corndon Tor are off the top of the hill to the east. It is from here, as well as from the cairns, that yet another wide variety of Dartmoor scenery can be looked upon, both the wilder regions to the north-west and south, plus the softer river valleys to the east and south-west, to Dartmeet and beyond. A tall cross stands to the south-west; this is a memorial to a young Lieutenant Cave-Penney, who failed to return home from the First World War. A visit to the cross before ascending to Corndon Tor does not take too long as you can pull off the minor road from Ollsbrim Cross where the signpost to Sherril is followed; the cross is a few metres off the road to the right.

COSDON BEACON — Belstone/Taw — 636915 — 550 — R T
Cawsand [SR]
Cosdonne Hill [SR]
Cairns on the summit and 150 m N of the highest point. Also used as a beacon in 1977, the Silver Jubilee of Queen Elizabeth II. In Jones' book, it is said that at 1792 ft according to the Trigonometrical Survey (Board of Ordnance), the hill was the highest part of Dartmoor.

COX TOR — Tavistock — 531762 — 442 — M R T
Cocks Tor [C] + [J] + [EH]
Gt Staple Tor 1.25 km E; Roos Tor 1.5 km ENE; Vixen Tor 2 km SE; Pew Tor 2.5 km S.
Coxtor is also the name of an old house, typical of the manor house of the 14th or 15th century. It is 1 km to the west of the trig. point along the walled enclosures between the tor and the valley of the Collybrook. On the top, many low, scattered piles of rock appear in profusion with many cairns, evidence of the popularity of the tor with prehistoric folk!
Superb views over Cornwall beyond Tavistock make the walk to the top well worth the effort as many people have found; often on Sunday afternoons, cars are left at Pork Hill as their occupants walk steadily uphill, northwards for 1.5 km.

CRAMBER TOR — Meavy — 584712 — 420 — R
Black Tor 1 km NW; Hart Tor 1 km NNW; also the tors above Burrator and around the quarries on the Princetown railway are visible to the west and north. Hart Tor Brook N; R. Meavy W; Newleycombe Brook S across the monk's path.
This is a solid, single mass of granite, easily climbed but too often littered with rubbish, especially the plain bronze-coloured tins issued to the services and cadet groups. Looming above as you approach from the west and north, from the east the tor is not apparent until within 150 m.
The most pleasant walk to the tor starts at the small parking place laid down in 1988, on the B3212 about 2 km from Princetown where Black Tor is on the horizon 200 m SW. Either go to the tor or head for the valley where Black Tor Falls (q.v.) trickle or rage over the rocks. Cramber Tor, seen from the car park, appears when climbing southwards from the falls. A slight deviation to the east when crossing Hart Tor Brook leads you straight to Cramber Tor. A different route begins at Norsworthy Bridge, goes up the track eastwards in the woods to a gate, just after which a deep gully is seen north of the track. A narrow path up the right-hand side of this leads you to Crazywell Pool. From here, go north to cross Devonport Leat by bridge and head north, still following on a worn, narrow path until Cramber Tor comes into sight a little to the left on the ridge.

CREBER'S ROCK see Claret Tor
CRIP TOR — Walkham — 555727 — c.280
Ingra Tor 600 m S; R. Walkham 1.25 km W; Yes Tor Brook 100 m S.
Two low piles are found to the west of the farm and these make up Crip Tor. A bridlepath passes to the south-east crossing the brook on open moor. Difficult to access from the east as Yes Tor Brook slowly flows through a boggy area.

CRIPDON DOWN TORS — Widecombe — 733805 — 360 — M
Hayne Down 1.5 km E; Nattadon Tor 7 km NNW; King Tor (hill above) 2 km NW.
The main pile is a substantial group of rocks about 3 m high on the western side with a second height 50 m to the north, this with a grassy covering. A third outcrop complete with logan stone is seen 250 m to the NE. These tors are about 400 m N of Jays Grave, on the eastern side of the road.

CROCKERN TOR — W. Dart — 616758 — c.400 — R
Littaford Tors 1.25 km N; Bellever Tor 3 km ENE; N. Hessary Tor 4 km WSW; Gt Mis Tor 5.5 km WNW.
According to Risdon, a writer in the early 17th century, this is one of Dartmoor's "remarkable" things (the others being Childe's Tomb, near Fox Tor, and Wistman's Wood under Longaford Tor). Remarkable it may be, but only in a historical sense; this tor was the seat of the Stannary Parliament, a group of representatives of the tin-miners. At each sitting twenty-four men were sent to the tor from each of the quarters based at Chagford, Ashburton, Plympton and Tavistock

(the stannary towns). Records began, as far as we know, in 1494, and many stories can be read of their exploits and decisions in other publications. The last meeting was held here in 1796, but even before this date, the tinners usually adjourned to the more comfortable surroundings in Tavistock. Crockern Tor was chosen because it was (is?) the geographical centre of the moor, a similar distance from those four towns. To visit this tor, stop at the stile near Parson's Cottage on the B3212, walk 200 m N up to the top of the hill.

CROW TOR   W. Dart   607788   c.500   R

Rough Tor 1 km N; Longaford Tor 1 km SE; Beardown Tor 1.5 km S; Lydford Tor 1 km SW; W. Dart 350 m E; Foxholes Brook 200 m W.

A single stack which, with some stretch of the imagination, could be seen as a bird's beak from the distant south or north. This tor held one of the first sixteen letterboxes and this one moves from the crack at the south-facing base to the top of the rock and back again depending on how the finder feels at the time. Approach Crow (sometimes pronounced to rhyme with "cow") Tor from the park at Two Bridges. Walk up the worn path past Wistman's Wood, over the stile and the Dart, and come to the tor after 4 km from the road. Seen from near the wood, you shouldn't go far wrong.

CROWNHILL TOR   Lee Moor   575608   215   O

Whitehill Tor 600 m N; Blackalder Tor 1 km NW; most of the moor to the north is hidden behind the spoil tips of the china clay works; Torrycombe Brook N and W.

An unexciting tor with rather small rocks on the hilltop.

CUMSDON TOR see Combestone Tor

CUMSTON TOR see Combestone Tor

CURNEN TOR see Corndon Tor

DANNAGOAT TOR see Dunnagoat Tor, Higher

DEVILS TOR   Cowsic   597797   549   R
Devil Tor [BG]

Rough Tor 1 km ENE; Beardown Tor 2.5 km SSE; Conies Down Tor 1 km SW; Gt Mis Tor 4.5 km SW; Fur Tor 3.5 km NNW; Cowsic R. 500 m W; Summer Brook 500 m NW via peat workings.

William Crossing describes this as "not much of a tor"; he is correct up to a point but the walls of the tor are about 2 m high.

Beardown Man, the tall standing stone 30 m to the west, is one of the mysteries of Dartmoor in that no-one can be positive of its purpose. It is a fine needle-like monolith, but it is neither connected with a stone row nor a circle and it does not signify an ancient trackway across the moor. But there are other menhirs of similar character, such as Harbourne Man. Although this tor is some way from any road, the route to it is fairly simple: stop at Holming Beam (see Conies Down Tor), make your way north to the stream, go right to the confluence with the Cowsic at Traveller's Ford where the Lich way crosses the river. By walking at an angle to make the climb easier, you are also going towards the tor which will appear at about the same time as Beardown Man depending on the angle of approach.

18

DEWERSTONE ROCK   Shaugh Prior   538639   c.217

A mecca for rock-climbers, the highest cliff is over 50 m high. On the summit, the southernmost point of Wigford Down, are the remains of an Iron-age hill-fort (see Hunter's Tor, near Lustleigh), the ditches and walls now only like shallow waves on the ocean. Crossing writes the name as Dewer Stone when writing of the rock as one of his 'Gems' of Dartmoor.

DINGER TOR   W. Okement   587881   c.550   H

Steeperton Tor 3.25 ENE; Gt Kneeset 2.25 km S; Lints Tor 850 m SW; Gt Links Tor 4 km WSW; Stenga Tor 1.75 km W; Black Tor 2.5 km NW; High Willhays 1.5 km NNW; W. Okement 1 km SW; Lints Tor Brook 200 m W; Brim Brook 500 m E and SE.

Yet another flat-topped pile into which the army shed has been installed. Dinger Tor is at the end of a stony track which runs South from near Row Tor. You may be stopped if the services are around so, to visit this rather inconspicuous location, start from the observation post No 15 (GR 602878) and walk 1.5 km WNW. The terrain is rougher in this part of the moor – none of the golf-course type short turf which is met with in other areas but, after all, you can't always have it easy! Dinger Tor is the scene of the legend of Blunderbus (no I'd never heard of it either) which is found in Tom Gant's *Dartmoor Legends Retold*.

DOE TOR   Lyd   542848   425   M P R

Brat Tor 800 m NNW; Sharp Tor 900 m E; Hare Tor 1 km SE; Brentor 8.5 km SW; Doe Tor Brook 200 m N; Wallabrook 300 m S.

Many remains of the efforts of the tinners are seen in these parts; in Foxholes, in the valley of Doe Tor Brook, the mine called Wheal Frederick was once a thriving place. The relics here include a wheel-pit, an oblong building which could have housed the miners overnight, a dry leat channel

and many heaps of spoil upstream of the ruin. A search of the tor and Foxholes can be made by starting the route at High Down (see Brat Tor), follow the Lyd down to the Doe Tor Brook, which comes in from the left (east), turn to go up the side of the brook for 1 km and turn right to the rocks.

DOWN TOR   Deancombe   580694   +346   M R

Combeshead 1 km SE; Newlycombe Lake N; Narrator Brook S.

Good views over Burrator to the west and to the little-known Snappers Tor to the WSW. Down Tor is exactly on the 4°W Longitude. Burrator Forest, established in 1921 to enhance the scenery around the newly created reservoir, should have set a life-long precedent in making a greener, softer environment around such waters but someone forgot to plant any trees, let alone conifers, around Meldon and Avon Dam Reservoirs. A walk of 1.25 km E from Norsworthy Bridge, through some enclosure walls, will bring you to the tor passing Snappers Tor on the right.

DUNNAGOAT TOR, HGR   Rattlebrook   558865   560   nr K R
Dannagoat Tor [SR]

Gt Links Tor 750 m NW; Green Tor 400 m E; Hunt Tor 1 km N; Lower Dunnagoat Tor 100 m S; Rattlebrook E with Bleak House in the valley below.

A boundary stone to the south-west delineates the Okehampton and Bridestowe/Sourton parishes, but the original Forest of Dartmoor boundary was the left bank of Rattlebrook with the water as the border. See Lower Dunnagoat Tor for access.

DUNNAGOAT TOR, LWR   Rattlebrook   558863   550   nr **K M**
Higher Dunnagoat Tor 100 m N; Green Tor 400 m N of E; Rattlebrook E; Doe Tor Brook SW.
A more impressive outcrop than its neighbour, with two main outcrops.
From High Down, go between Arms Tor and Brat Tor. From the footbridge over the R. Lyd, go 2.5 km until track begins to descend and keep uphill to the left, walking north-east for 250 m to Lower Dunnagoat.

EASDON TOR   Manaton   729823   439   **M R T**
East Down Tor [SR]
Eastdon Tor [SR]
Hunters Tor, on R. Bovey, 3 km E; Hayne Down 2.5 km SE; Hameldon Tor 3 km SW.
On the hill, the piles dominate the summit but there is another outcrop 350 m E, past the cairn. A row of stones which run at a zig-zag east to west denote the boundary between the parishes of Manaton and North Bovey. Easdon Tor is best reached on foot from Manaton, but a narrow lane runs past Barracott to a gate. There are no passing places so after reading this, all you millions

of people should leave your transport somewhere else. This tor is uphill all the way (of course!).

EAST MIL see Mill Tor, East

EAST TOR   Sourton   539897   370   **R**
A misnomer, as it's *west* of the main tors on Sourton's rocky outpost, as well as being on the north-west edge of Dartmoor. From Sourton Church, go uphill to the most southerly of the line of outcrops; no other tors are visible, apart from the other Sourton Tors.

EAST TOR [c]   Walkham   564725
Yes Tor [c] + **[Dartmoor National Park]**
200 m W of Fur Tor, overlooking the Plymouth and Dartmoor tramway or, strictly speaking, where it once was; Yes Tor Brook to the N; Leeden Tor is 750 m S; Ingra Tor 1 km W; Swell Tor N. Reach from Princetown via Swell Tor or from the B3212 after Ingra Tor.

EASTDON TOR see Easdon Tor

EASTERN TOR   Plym   585665   333   **M R**
East Tor [SR]
Shavercombe Tor 1 km SE; Hen Tor 1.5 km SSE; Trowlesworthy Tors 2 km S; Gutter Tor 1 km NW; R. Plym E and S; Gutter Mire W; Drizzlecombe 1 km E.
Here is the most impressive collection of stone rows, monoliths and cairns on the moor, and that includes Merrivale. The tallest standing stone is over 4 m high, and the second tallest is a few

paces away. The stone rows are double lines of short stones leading to (but not continuously) burial mounds above them. Giant's Basin, a large barrow to the east of the tallest stone has been rifled over the years and is now a hollow filled with many pale grey stones. (Cairns are of rocks; barrows of earth-coverings.) To the south-west of the western pile of the tor stands Ditsworthy Warren House. Not so long ago, the RAF used the building as a training base for cadets. A leat feeds water directly into the house and there are slight rises in the lawn, called pillow-mounds, artificial bunny-homes; the animals were made to feel at ease in these humps, creating an atmosphere where they could procreate. In the corner of one of the walled fields is a stone kennel where dogs could guard against intruders, both of two and four legs, and to aid Fido in the latter, vermin-traps were operated (see Legis Tor). Warrens were established at Headland, under Birch Tor, Vaghill near Sharp Tor over Dartmeet and Longaford Tor which looks down on the site of Wistman's Warren. There were at least fifteen on the moor at one time. Access from Burcombe, under Gutter Tor, along the stony track on the west side of mire, crossing over the bridge, then south-east.

EFFORTHER see Hessary Tor, North

ELSFORD ROCK	**Lustleigh**	**786830**	**290**	**E X**
EMSWORTHY ROCKS [EH]	**Haytor**	**752769**	**+400**	**Q R**

These lie on the north side of the ridge, north of Saddle Tor and just south of west from Haytor. They are seen on the horizon between the two tors, when looking from the road.

ERNESTORRE see Yes Tor

EYLESBARROW TOR   **Plym**   **599686**   **454**

[B] says that Eylesbarrow (he spells it "Eylesburgh") is a tor of no very great altitude. (Local pronunciation is "Yelsboro".) The writer is correct in one respect: the rocks are quite low, so low, in fact, that you would hardly know they're there. The tallest stones are on two cairns and the nearby grassy wall. As far as altitude goes, the hill commands an all-round view of most of the south-west moor. An interesting feature is seen to the WSW of the summit: near the line of tall PCWW stones, to their right going downhill, is a row of double stones about 6 m apart. They were used to support a flat rod system of driving machinery at the mine by way of the large water-wheel beyond the site of Wheal Ruth near the flattening out of the hill roughly 600 m away. The supports are only half-a-metre high, and they bear the blackish stains of lubricant which was necessary to maintain smooth working, especially in the damp conditions in this exposed place. The summit of Eylesbarrow is reached by a long, but easy, stroll from South Hessary Tor (q.v.) and Nun's Cross, staying on the hard-packed growan path SSW rising gradually on the way. Apart from the number of PCWW stones, you will see rougher markers; these are the boundary stones of the forest of Dartmoor (Lydford parish) and Walkhampton parish, although no lettering can be traced on any of them.

FEATHER TOR   **Walkham**   **535741**   **313**   **R**

Vixen Tor 700 m E; Pew Tor 700 m SSW; R. Walkham to the east 1 km; Grimstone and Sortridge Leat flows from the north and passes the tor to the west.

Windy Post, a slightly leaning granite cross is north-west of Feather Tor on the bank of the leat, and overlooks an example of a bulls-eye stone. These ensured a constant and fair supply of water to habitations below a leat and this hole in a granite block is one of many on this leat.
The tor consists of low piles of rock made into one flat lump by a grassy covering and a few trees.
From Pork Hill car park it is 1 km SSE across an area reminiscent of a well-kept fairway.

FIGGIE DANIEL   **North Bovey**   **735823**   **c.425**

Found about 300 m SE of the trig. point on Easdon Tor. Included because of its shape and prominence, similar to but shorter than Bowerman's Nose and among other large boulders. It is probably on the boundary between the parishes of North Bovey and Manaton: it should be, anyway!

FLAT TOR   **Dart**   **609815**   **c.540**

(GR 608817 acc. to Helen Harris)
Rough Tor 1.5 km W of S; Kit Rocks 1.25 km NNE; Broad Down 3.5 km ESE; East Dart R. 600 m NE; West Dart R. 400 m W and S.

A 1.5 m high cliff which runs around the south and east of the tor and one or two low boulders is all that this site offers. However, flat it certainly is and more of a tor than the position marked by the OS map's 603807, where only a 2 m boulder near an unnamed tributary of Summer Brook could possibly warrant the use of the word 'tor'. On the summit of the grassy pile is the range notice board which is marked by the OS at this site. To gain access to this more remote spot, a route including the heights to the east of the West Dart takes you to Brown's House via Hr White Tor, then over Wildbanks Hill to the north and thence NNW avoiding the slight depressions on either side. Often this is very marshy, but Flat Tor is visible from the hill.

FOGGIN TOR   Walkham   567735   c.400   Q R
Fogging Tor [SR]

I've cheated here! No tor as such now exists but before extensive quarrying began, there was a tor on the ridge above what is now a sheer cliff. Suppose many other Dartmoor landmarks were removed in like manner – no Yes Tor, Hollow Tor would be completely empty, and if South Hessary disappeared, Hessary Tor would revert to its original name.

Approach to this site is easier from Four Winds car park, and an easy stroll past Yellowmead Farm to the south-east brings you to a track which passes the quarry on your left. A few relics of the industry are still standing, but be warned against using them as anything other than something to look at: they are unstable even in calm weather.

FOX TOR   Mary Tavy   514788   190   N F R ptW
High Tor 200 m SW; Kents Tor 500 m NE; R. Tavy flows E–S through a steep-sided valley.

Seen on the ridge among trees from the footpath and field east of Mary Tavy church, Fox Tor is one of five less-famous outcrops which stand on the west bank of the Tavy between Horndon Bridge and Peter Tavy.

FOX TOR   Swincombe   626698   438   M R
Lt Fox Tor 500 m W; Foxtor mire to the north; R. Swincombe to the east.

To visit this one, park off the road from Princetown to Whiteworks (i.e. Castle Lane), follow the leat to or towards Nun's Cross Farm then turn to the tor which is 2 km from the farm and visible from the road. Foxtor Farm is 800 m NNE and is the setting of Eden Phillpotts's novel, *The American Prisoner*. Only a few walls are left and not a trace of the cellar which featured in the book. Almost due north of the tor is Childe's Tomb about which every other Dartmoor book has a few words to say. No sign of blood remains and the bones have been removed!

FOX TOR, LITTLE   Swincombe   621698   420   M
Yonder Tor

Foxtor Mire due N; Childe's Tomb 500 m NE. From Nun's Cross, less than 2 km E.

FOXWORTHY TOR [C]   Lustleigh   761821   c.300   M
Raven's Tor 250 m SSE; Hunters Tor 450 m N.

For access, follow your choice of route to Ravens Tor, then follow the contour NNW to the tor, which is in fact a scattering of large rocks.

FRENCHBEER ROCK   Teign   671854   387
Frenchbeer Tor [C]
Frenchbere Tor [SR]

Thornworthy Tor 750 m WSW; Middle Tor is halfway between Kes and Frenchbeer Rocks; S. Teign 350 m E running NNE.

Take the road from Chagford towards Kestor Rock. At Yeo, go south toward Teignworthy Hotel. Keep on the road to an unfenced stretch on the right and Frenchbeer Rock is 100 m from the road.

FUR TOR   Tavy   588830   572   M R
Vurtorre [C] from Saxon word 'far' = distant, or Celtic 'efford' = path or from 'fawr' = great. All may equally apply to this most remote tor, which was once close to a route across the moor from east to west.

Hare Tor 4 km WNW; Gt Links Tor 5 km NW; High Willhays 6 km N; Sittaford Tor 4.5 km E, but not quite visible from ground level; Pole above Lynch Tor 3.5 km S of SW; Fur Tor Brook 1 km S and W; Cut Combe Water 400 m E and N.

The "Queen of the Tors" consists of ten or twelve piles of granite over a wide area, many of which are over 10 m high. Large amounts of clitter cover the north and west slopes. The group of four outcrops to the east show good examples of lamellar bedding of granite (thin layers in a sliced loaf formation). A hundred metres to the west of this group is the largest pile of the tor, in block granite. The other 'torlets' are to the west of the major pile. Access is easy, if not strenuous; from Lane End (GR 537823) go east to meet Mine Leat, follow it to its source in Tavy Cleave. Keep on west bank of the Tavy through the cleave for 3 km till tor is ahead and east. Cross Amicombe Brook where convenient (depends on the speed of flow) and head uphill to the tor.

FUR TOR Walkham 565725 320 M

Leeden Tor 1 km S.

Overlooks a tight bend in the former Plymouth and Dartmoor railway. Fur Tor is mentioned by Hemery in *Walking the Dartmoor Railroads* and also was the site of a "letterbox" which carried the name. Access by the track from Princetown cutting across the moor before reaching Foggintor, or from Sharpitor car park (GR 560709), go 2 km NNE.

GER TOR Tavy 547831 430 H M P R
Great Tor [SR] + [BA]

Hare Tor 1 km NNE; Brat Tor 2.5 km NNW; Brent Tor 8 km WSW; Nat Tor 700m S; Tavy Cleave Tors 800 m E; R. Tavy flows on the east to the south sides and Reddaford (Mine Leat on some OS maps). Leat contours the slope on south and west of tor. Willsworthy Brook is 1.25 km W. The leat is remarkable in the fact that in 7 km, the drop is only 4 m: some feat in the days before computers.
The mine in question was Wheal Jewel, now a serpentine reservoir. Another leat from the Tavy above Hill Bridge (GR 532804) flows above the west bank, through Kents Tor (q.v.) and enters a small reservoir before running to the power station at Mary Tavy. Ger Tor can be visited from Lane End, near Willsworthy from which it is 1 km NE.

GIBBY COMBE TOR Holy Brook 678686 320

No other tor is visible from this one as it sits in a valley facing south-west overlooking two stones which form the boundary between Buckfast and Holne.

GIDLEIGH TOR Teign 672878 334 N F R

Meldon Tor 2.5 km SE; Easdon Tor nearly 8 km SE; Haytor over 13 km S of SE; Hameldown Tor 8 km SSE; Kes Tor 1.5 km SSW; North Teign 300 m S.
Gidleigh Tor is one of those out-of-the-way areas which few explorers of Dartmoor seem to visit. Covered with gorse and moss, the rock stands around 5 m at its highest part; two very low outcrops accompany the main tor. Thirty metres to the west of the tor is a strange, round, roofless building. This is Princep's folly, which was supposedly erected as a look-out point for Mr and Mrs Princep. It is hardly a folly: anyone with the time and planning permission to build a house with such a panorama can not be said to be foolish, quite the opposite. The rotunda is 4 m or so in diameter, but its walls are home for thick strands of ivy. Gidleigh Chase, the area of woodland on the banks of the Teign, is another 'Gem' and from Batworthy to Holystreet, there are 4 km of almost unbroken mixed woodland.

GNATS' HEAD, LITTLE Plym 608674 410

Calveslake Tor due N; opposite Harter Tors on the other bank of the Plym, Deadman's Bottom S; Langcombe Brook 700 m SW.
On N T ground, this really is a small tor – low piles of granite not too different from the tor to the north. In that direction, in 100 m, is a good example of a kist or cist or kistvaen (stone-chest), level with the ground and about 900 mm x 600 mm x 500 mm deep, its four slabs making an open box. Due west of the rocks, on the bank of the Plym, are the remains of a blowing-house.

GRADNER ROCKS Lustleigh 781802 178

On the edge of Hisley Wood and almost due south of the village, nearly 2 km by footpath which leads directly below the rocks.

GREA TOR see Smallacombe Rocks

GREAT HOUND TOR see Hound Tor

GREAT KING TOR see King's Tor

GREAT KNEESET	W. Okement	589859	567	**M R**

A high elevation but not an outstanding feature in the impressive stakes. Some of the worst terrain for walking on is to the west, with peat-hags, wide pools and high turfs, and long climbing grass. To the east, there's a slight improvement in the going, and if you can negotiate the ground, Cranmere Pool will be reached after 1.5 km. Kneeset itself has a flattish, grassy top on the more elevated northern rocks.

GREAT ROCK	Bovey Tracey	827815		**X**

Site of a mine which was operated from 1805 to 1969.

GREAT ROOSE TOR see Staple Tor, Great

GREAT TOR see Ger Tor

GREATOR ROCKS	Manaton	748787	371	**M R W**

Grea Tor [C]

Leighon Tor [SR]

Haytor 2 km SSE; Rippon Tor 3 km S; Chinkwell Tor 2 km WSW; Smallacombe Rocks (Grea Tor) 800 m SE; Hayne Down 1.5 km N.

Quite an impressive line of fairly sharp tors which run north-east to south-west, supporting much vegetation, especially on the west faces; small trees (holly, rowan) and moss add to its beauty. On the east side is a rock-basin often found on tors with flat rocks, but Greator Rocks are composed of large slanting slabs and make the outline more dramatic than many other tors. Approach via Hound Tor (q.v.)

GREEN TOR	Rattlebrook	561864	540	nr **K**

Kitty Tor 1.5 km NE; Fur Tor 4 km SSE; Hare Tor 2.5 km SW; Higher Dunnagoat 400 m W; Gt Links Tor 1 km WNW; Rattlebrook 200 m W; Green Tor Water 200 m SE.

Green Tor overlooks Bleak House, a favourite objective for navigation and expedition groups and unfortunately used by some as a dumping ground for litter. A bad example was set by the military some years ago when the house was used as a target for shell-firing. In the more pleasant past, it was said to be the home of the manager of the peat-works.

These remains are found a few hundred paces up the valley and the peat-hags extend over many acres between here and Kitty Tor. The track of the former railway gives a relatively easy route to this area; the track and the workings have been used intermittently up to as late as the early 1950s, but all of the more recent ventures have been failures to some degree or other. Access to Green Tor is either from Sourton Church (GR 536903), Sourton Tors and, by walking towards Gt Links Tor – the most prominent outcrop to the south – you meet the track. Follow it to its terminus at a bridge, cross it, turn south to Bleak House and the tor is just above to the east. Alternatively, park at High Down car park, cross the R. Lyd by bridge, pass between Brat Tor (with the cross) and Arms Tor to the left, walk eastwards until you descend into Rattlebrook Valley and bear half left to see the tor ahead and Bleak House below. By this route you cross the boundary of the ancient Forest of Dartmoor. The perambulation of the 'Forest' follows in part the Lydford parish bounds and you may notice a stone on a path near the highest point of this approach. It is inscribed "L" for Lydford and the 1239-40 line was Rattlebrook itself, a few hundred metres away.

GREN TOR	Lyd	551880	510	

Grenny [EH]

Sourton Tors 2 km NNW; Hunt Tor 700 m SE; Gt Links Tor 1.25 km S; Lt Links Tor 1.25 km SSW; Arms Tor 2 km SSW; R. Lyd 200 m N then W.

This tor is one rock mass about 30 m long but doesn't rise above 3 m high. Like Green Tor you can approach this from Sourton. After crossing the Lyd at Lydda Bridge (on the Rattlebrook railway track), Gren Tor is to the left on the slope. The views are more impressive than the tor itself and, given the right conditions, Bodmin Moor can be clearly seen on the horizon. Just to the east of the rocks, a gully marks the original path which the peat workers used from the north-western settlements to the peat hags on Amicombe Hill. Packhorses laden with blocks of peat made their way via Hunt Tor to the bridge and thence to the various destinations. The railway opened in 1878 and since then the older route to the peat-works has become marshy and, in places, impassable.

GRENES TOR see Yes Tor
GRIMS TOR see Hameldown Tor

GUTTER TOR	**Plym**	**577668**	**350**	**M R** (to sw)**T**

Eastern Tor 1 km SE; Hen Tor 2.25 km SE; Whittenknowles Rocks due E; R. Plym 1 km S; Gutter Mire E; Nattor Brook rises in Gutter Mire and runs to the east and north.

A much visited tor being so close to the lane and on hand for visitors to the Ditsworthy Training Centre, marked "Scout Hut" on the map, which was renovated in 1989. The views from here have been completely spoiled by the erection in the mid-80s of wire fences which surround Ringmoor Down in its entirety. Although a short climb takes you from your car to the tor, a longer walk to, say, Legis Tor or Ringmoor Cottage, necessitates climbing over stiles or following the fences around the higher parts of the down.

HALL TOR see Tristis Rock

HAMELDOWN TOR	**Widecombe**	**702806**	**529**	**R T**

Grims Tor [C]
Hamilton Tor [J]

A few large boulders; cairn on the summit; Hookney Tor 850 m NNW; King Tor 1.25 km NNE; Birch Tor 2 km NW; Chinkwell Tor 3.5 km SE; Bellever Tor 7 km SW; West Webburn 1 km W; Grimslake 400 m N.

The tor overlooks Grimspound, the most famous of Dartmoor's many ancient settlements and one which, like Childe's Tomb, has been written about countless times, so it only remains for it to be said that William Crossing counts Grimspound as one of his 'Gems', and enjoy the views from the tor itself. In fact, once you have made the ascent from the road, an easy walk along the ridge going south leads you to a line of inscribed stones put up at the instigation of the Duke of Somerset, which marks the bounds of Natsworthy. Four stones in the 'set' are on the ridge, others are between Broad Barrow and Natsworthy Gate. Nearly all have their own names, as do those mentioned under Grea Tor.

HAMPSTER TOR	**W. Okement**	**580893**	**610**	**R**

High Willhayes 350 m S; Yes Tor 300 m NE; Branscombe's Loaf 3 km SW.

100 m W of the track between the two highest points in Devon, making it the third highest tor on Dartmoor with more great views to the west. Another example of lamellar bedding.

HANGERSHELL ROCK	**Erme**	**654594**	**350**

Hanger's Shil [B]
Hangershiel Rock [EH]

Three Barrows 3 km N; Eastern Whittaburrow 6 km E of N; Butterdon Hill 700 m S; Pen Beacon 6.5 km NW; Stalldon 3.5 km NNW; Sharp Tor 2.5 km W of N.

A closely grouped, tor-like feature with a clear shelf of granite when seen from the west. In the 19th century, horse-racing took place on the short, springy turf.

HANGINGSTONE HILL	**Taw head**	**617861**	**603**	**H P R**

Army huts are on the summit, next to a low grassy bank on granite 'walls'. Much erosion by boots has made the area less attractive. The 'Hanging Stone' is some way to the north-west, an obvious formation of three or four large rocks, one of which sticks out and up from its companion.

HARE TOR [C]	**Wapsworthy**	**553803**	**c.390**

On page 173 of his *Guide to Dartmoor*, Crossing says that Hare Tor is "above Wapsworthy Wells" which are themselves "above Longbetor" (p. 169). The only feature remotely resembling a tor is a low rock-pile about 4 m in diameter seen over the wall beyond a gate close to the two green army huts along the track from Wapsworthy Gate, near Bagga Tor. The pile looks as though it could be an artificial heap made by a bulldozer, but no other feature is in sight. This, therefore, is likely to be the tor to which Crossing refers.

HARE TOR   Tavy   55184   521   P R

Sharp Tor 600 m N; Gt Links Tor 2.5 km N; Chat Tor 1.25 km NNE; Kitty Tor nearly 4 km NNE; Fur Tor 3.5 km ESE; Ger Tor 1 km SSW; Doe Tor 1 km NW; R. Tavy 1 km SE and S; Willsworthy Brook 1 km SW; Deadlake 600 m E flowing E.

A fine conical tor with trees growing around the base, and among the lower rocks, with a large amount of grass on all sides forming terraces for people with packed lunches to rest while enjoying the scene. It's one of my favourite tors in my favourite part of Dartmoor and, apart from the views over the wilderness, a wide area of Cornwall is seen, including the TV mast on Caradon

Hill, 30 km SW. A not too strenuous walk from Lane End to Tavy Cleave can be undertaken, up the Rattlebrook, NW up Deadlake to the WD stone and the cairn due north of the tor. Then gently climb up to the summit of Hare Tor for the panorama before finally dropping down by way of the old rails of the mobile target on Willsworthy Range above Reddaford Leat to Lane End. The more direct way is the opposite: Hare Tor is seen from the parking area and, providing the marshy patches near Willsworthy Brook are avoided, the walk is easy, if up hill, all the way.

HARE TOR, LITTLE [c]   Tavy   546842   445   M

Ger Tor 1 km S; Brentor 8.5 km WSW; Doe Tor 800 m NW; Brat Tor 1.5 km NNW; Wallabrook 500 m NW; Willsworthy Brook 300 m SW.

There is a striking view of these rocks from below when you approach Hare Tor; a flat, single pile seems to be the character of this tor when seen from above, or east. Hare Tor is 300 m east of this.

HART TOR   Meavy   581720   390   M R
Harter Tor [sr]

Cramber Tor 800 m SSE; Black Tor 1 km WSW; South Hessary Tor 1.5 km ENE; R. Meavy 300 m W; Hart Tor Brook 300 m SW.

Due north from the middle of the tor you may find small upright stone posts with figures on the top. These are the distances from a former rifle range shown on some OS maps. If you head towards the TV mast, they are within a few paces of your path. To gain access to Hart Tor, stop at the first milestone from Princetown on the Yelverton Road (SE), then walk 1 km due south, through some clitter straight to the tor.

HART TOR [c]   Okehampton   603918   436   H R W

Belstone Tor 1.5 km NE; Oke Tor 1.5 km SE; East Mill Tor 1.25 km S; Yes Tor 2.25 km SW; West Mill Tor 1.25 km W; Row Tor 1 km NW; E. Okement R. 500 m E; Blackaven Brook 250 m W.

Due west of the rocks is one of Okehampton's parish boundary stones, on the bank of the Blackaven next to a shallower part of that brook called Middle Ford. The tor itself is one pile of layered granite and is next to the 'ring road', south of the fork, on the south-west corner of East Okement Farm.

HARTER TOR, HIGHER   Plym   600677   410   R

Calveslake Tor 800 m E; Gt Gnats Head 2.5 km E; Gutter Tor 2.5 km WSW; Down Tor 2.5 km NW; Sharpitor and Leather Tor about 5 km NE; Leeden Tor 5.5 km between Down Tor and Sharpitor; Sheepstor 3.5 km NNW; Gt Staple Tor 10 km NNW with White Tor 13 km to the right of Staple Tor; Brent Tor is seen 19 km away NW; R. Plym E and S 600 m distant.

These rocks are only visible from the mining remains on the track from the scout hut under Gutter Tor to Nun's Cross. You would not even suspect any size tor at all unless you approach to within a hundred metres and then the tor becomes apparent. From the hut, walk up the track towards Eylesbarrow to the ruins of Wheal Ruth, over two kilometres, then turn SSE and walk to the tor.

HARTER TOR, LOWER   Plym   600675   c.390   M

Calveslake Tor 600 m N of E; Little Gnats Head 500 m ESE; Hen Tor 2.5 km SSW; Gt Trowlesworthy 4 km SW; Lt Trowlesworthy to the right of it; Legis Tor 4 km to the right again; R. Plym flows E and S; Langcombe Brook runs towards you from the S.

This tor is more impressive than its higher namesake; there is one large stack and, to the south-west, many smaller ones, all contriving to give the idea that these two tors are the wrong way around! Higher Harter Tor is 300 m NW.

HARTLAND TOR   Postbridge   641799   410   M

Stannon Tor 1.25 km NNE; Bellever Tor 3.5 km S; East Dart R. runs NW to S; Braddon Lake comes from the W into the Dart.

The highest part of the tor has a grassy top, but on the south and west sides there are sheer walls which need care when looking for a way down. Hartland Hill, as [BA] calls it, overlooks one of the ancient tenements of the moor, mentioned in early records of freeholdings and tenancy; several of the neighbouring farms are equally as old or older. Close to the path, to the north-west, roughly 150 m from the summit, is a memorial to a Liverpool-based teacher who went missing on the moor. He left only a brief note to his family, giving no details as to his destination. It was three months before his body was found.

To get to this tor, start at Postbridge's main car park. Cross the Dart, preferably by the clapper bridge to avoid being hit by speeding vehicles, and walk up the waymarked path making a left-angled turn near Ringhill. Walk up the river keeping Hartland on right. Ascend after the newtake.

HARTON CHEST   Lustleigh   767818   260   R

A large cuboid rock resting on another, to the west of the path which comes up from Lustleigh and goes north-west along the ridge to Hunter's Tor.

HAWKS' TOR   Lee Moor   554625   270   M

Saddlesborough 750 m NE; Crownhill Tor 2.5 km SE; Shaugh Beacon; 1.25 km NW.

Although a comparatively small tor, Hawks' Tor is in its own way unique, almost forming a cave with its slab-like rocks. They are seen clearly from the road north of Beatland Corner, being on the skyline, and it is from a point 250 m SE of the crossroads that you can visit the rocks. Just walk 500 m NNE; the tor borders the china clay works. (See Collard Tor.)

HAYNE DOWN TORS   Manaton   742804(NW) 744801(SE)   c.420   R

Hound Tor 1.5 km S; Hunters Tor 2.5 km NE; Easdon Tor 2.5 km NNW.

Two large areas of scattered rocks each with a higher stack. Bowerman's Nose is below the NW group.

HAYTOR ROCKS   Bovey Tracey   758771   457   M R
Hey Tor [C] + [JC] + [EH]
High Tor [J] + [OLDER OS MAPS]

Saddle Tor 1 km SW; Rippon Tor 2 km SW; Chinkwell Tor 3 km WNW; Hound Tor 2.5 km NNW; Hunters Tor 5 km N; Bagtor 1.5 km E of S.

Arguably the most famous of Dartmoor's landmarks and certainly the most frequented due to its proximity to the road and ice-cream van/toilets. Rock climbers also use the high walls and years ago steps were hewn out to ease the climb to the top of the rock. I agree that it is a fine tor in its own right, but I feel that people miss the opportunity to get to know this part of the moor

by visiting Haytor again and again without going to one of the surrounding tors. I'm aware that some visitors are not physically able to walk further, but a stroll to Saddle Tor and Holwell Tor could start a craze. In this area one is never out of sight of the huge rocks and getting lost is such a remote possibility that it's unthinkable. Among the antiquities that can be missed are the granite railway to the north; quarries at Holwell Tor; quaries to the north-east of Haytor; and the Duke of Somerset's boundary stones on Haytor Down, again to the north. The quarry has a permanent pool which is excellent for watching pond life. Kingfishers have been seen here, perched on the rusty winch which was used to move the chunks of rock from the base of the face. The workings closed down in 1919 after the War Memorial was requisitioned for Exeter. Although not one of the 'Gems' named by William Crossing, he does tell of a legend, a love story, on page 84. Access, if necessary, is from the lower car park 600 m W; or from the higher, larger park (ices but no toilets!) 300 m N: you can't miss it!

HAZEL TOR see Ausewell Rocks

HECKWOOD TOR   Walkham   539737   321   Q R
Pew Tor 600 m WSW; Feather Tor 400 m NNW; Vixen Tor 700 m NE; King's Tor 2 km E; R. Walkham 1 km E.
The quarry (disused) is on the east side of the summit, near the track from Merrivale to Sampford Spiney. Approach Heckwood Tor from Pork Hill car park via Feather Tor. There is nothing of note about the tor itself, but there are fine views down the Walkham, across the valley towards King's Tor and Ingra Tor, to the south-east.

HELTOR ROCK   Teign   799870   310   E R W X
Hel Tor [JC]
Whitestone [SR]
Blackingstone Rock 2 km SW.
Access is gained from a footpath which runs from the lane at GR 800868.

HEMSTONE ROCKS   Teign   646835
These boulders are almost due east of Grey Wethers, inside the forest around Fernworthy Reservoir, but directions to them may vary as the tracks used by the Forestry Commission are liable to change depending on which area is cleared or reafforested. I reached the group by way of the gate entering the wood at the point where the infant South Teign goes into the wood. The track bent round from the north-east to north and, in 300 m, the rocks were on the left of the track in the small clearing.

HEN TOR   Plym   593653   414   M
Gt Trowlesworthy Tor (top of) 1.75 km SW; Legis Tor 2.25 km N of W; Gutter Tor 2.25 km NW; Eastern Tor 1.5 km NNW.
Extensive clitter on the slopes towards the site of Hen Tor Warren and Farm. The walls and banks are clearly visible and are passed if the route to the tor is made from Burcombe. From the west of

the Plym, Hen Tor appears to be a triangle of rocks but at the tor, the tallest piles are on the lower slopes almost hiding shorter outcrops to the east. Like many of the tors on the east bank of the Plym, Hen Tor is on land cared for by the National Trust.

HEN TOR, LITTLE [c]   Plym   5965

The likely pile of rock which Crossing refers to is that which is 30 m S of the main outcrop of Hen Tor, but there is a scattering of large rocks about 400 m NW of Hen Tor, which is more likely to be given this name.

HERNE HOLE TOR   Princetown   578744   495

N Hessary Tor 300 m S; Gt Mis Tor 3 km NNW; Rundlestone Tor 250 m NW. Other tors visible from North Hessary are also seen from here.

Now accessible via a stile in the wall north of N Hessary; two piles in scrubby vegetation and about 150 m from the wall.

HESSARY TOR, NORTH   Princetown   579742   51   K R T
Efforther [RISDON]
Hisworthie [SR]
Hisworthy Tor [C]
Ysfother [B]

In his *Guide to Dartmoor*, William Crossing lists numerous tors which can be seen from this "elevated spot" and, no doubt, on a clear day you could count up to 20 tors. You can even see the twin churches of St Marychurch in Torquay, over 32 km away! The two most prominent tors are Gt Mis Tor 3 km NNW and King's Tor 2 km S of W. The television mast was established in 1954. When it was first suggested that such an obtrusive object was to invade the Dartmoor landscape, cries of "shame" were heard across the region, but many a walker, me included, has always looked upon the mast as a friend, a waymark and a damned good point of reference whenever bad weather looms up. Access is either from the car park in Princetown itself (turn left, follow the footpath signs and go through the gate with the hill ahead) or from the telephone box at Rundlestone, from which the metalled road to the radio station is walked, passing Rundlestone Tor on your right as you ascend.

HESSARY TOR, SOUTH   Princetown   597723   45   K R W
Histworthy Tor [SR]
Little Hisworthie [SR]
Look-out Tor [C]
Tor Royal [SR]

Hart Tor Brook rises to the west and flows away from the tor past Hart Tor itself 1.5 km WSW.
The tor is prominent from many points to the south and west, not only because of its shape but also its position on the ridge between Foxtor Mire and Hart Tor Brook. There was a rusty metal spike on the tor of about 45 cm and I would like to think that it was once a support for a spyglass when Look-out Tor was used to watch for escaped prisoners-of-war from the prison buildings. To find South-Hessary, take the worn but made-up track between the Plume of Feathers and the Devil's Elbow, then find the old toilets at Princetown, pass between them then simply keep the wall on your left for 1.25 km. The track is called Ivybridge Lane.

HEXTON TOR   Plym   582637   c.370
Gt Trowlesworthy Tor 500 m NNW.
This consists of small piles of rocks overlooking china clay workings, between which runs a drainage ditch, nearly 2 miles long, contouring the slope under the tors and Pen Beacon.

HEY/HIGH TOR see Haytor Rocks

HIGH TOR   Tavy   512787   170   N W
Fox Tor 200 m NE; Longtimber Tor 500m SSW, but not visible.
The tor can be seen from the field above Mary Tavy Church, the footpath going through on the north side, and is 150 m away. The Tavy flows close by to the east, Cholwell Brook is 400 m W. High Tor is the second one going north-east from Peter Tavy between the village and Horndon Bridge.

HIGHER TOR   Belstone   612917   c.460   nr K R
Belstone Tor due N; Oke Tor 1.5 km S; Steeperton Tor 3 km S; E Mill Tor 2 km SW; Knattborough Tor 700 m SSW; Winter Tor 300m WSW.
The most southerly of the Belstone range of rocks, found by keeping to the ridge after seeing the other tors to the north. Nineteenth century maps show Higher Tor to be exactly that: the highest pile in the Belstone ridge some 200 m to the north of the present Higher Tor. A stone 250 m to the south is on the borders of Belstone and Lydford Parishes.

HIGHER WHITEN TOR see White Tor, Higher

HIGH WILLHAYS   Okehampton   580893   621   K M R
Hampster Tor [DONN:1765]
High Willes [C] + [EH]
Hight Will [C, QUOTING A 1532 SOURCE]
The highest point of the moor and, although crowned with some small piles of granite, Donn is the only writer to refer to the place as a tor. A cairn, which appears to grow each time I see it, has been built on one of the highest outcrops. Lamellar bedding is in evidence on all the piles, which are spread out from north to south on the ridge.

HINGSTON ROCKS   Moreton   769858   c.320   R W X
Ingstone Rock [SR]

HISTWORTHY TOR see Hessary Tor, South

HOCKINSTON TOR   Dart   695719   200

Hockington Tor, according to Samuel Rowe, can be reached by walking from Bel Tor Corner, along Dr Blackall's Drive to Mel Tor in 500 m, then along the edge of Meltor Wood (south-east of Mel Tor) then due south, steeply downhill. Bench Tor across the Dart due west.
The tor consists of two big, sloping slabs among clitter.

HOLE ROCK   Haytor   757785   c.360

Leighon Tor 250 m N; Smallacombe Rocks 250 m SSW; Greator Rocks 1 km W.
Immediately to the left of the path, going downhill from the saddle between Black Hill and Haytor Down, Hole Rock is used as a boundary marker for the former manors and present parishes (Ilsington and Manaton). A stone stands just below the tall rocks and is also used as a boundary-stone. It is one of a series of more interesting stones further uphill.

HOLLOW TOR   Princetown   571746   470   Q

Rundlestone Tor 500 m E; N Hessary Tor 800 m SW.
The quarry is on the north side and other diggings have taken place at ground level around this tor. Access from B3357 at Rundlestone Corner, up the footpath towards the mast, turn right to Rundlestone Tor then go west to Hollow Tor.

HOLLOW TOR   Widecombe   731762   365

Top Tor 500 m E; Pil Tor 450 m SE; Tunhill Rocks 450 m S; E. Webburn R. to W, with Widecombe 2 km away.
One of a number of tors to the east of the village, it could be included in the same walk. The "hollow" is made by a small pile separated from the main tor on the lower (west) side.

HOLWELL ROCKS   Widecombe   742783   390

William Crossing, in *Gems in a Granite Setting*, p 83, refers to the stack of rock on the east of the Hemsworthy Gate–Swallerton Gate road as Holwell Rocks, but there are few other, if any, mentions of the pile where walls meet; there are in fact, two separate piles, the higher one being at this junction. Other similar outcrops are found on the other side of the same road also on the summit of the hill, near Hedge Barton. A prehistoric "JCB" must have been busy in these parts.

HOLWELL TOR   Haytor   751776   402   Q R

Ovals Tor, a local name but only heard from the true moormen.
Smallacombe Rocks 600 m NNE; Haytor 800 m SE; Emsworthy Rocks 600 m S; Chinkwell Tor 2.5 km WNW; Becka Brook 500 m W.

The longest visible stretch of the Haytor granite railway starts below the tor, which has several relics from the age of quarrying lying around. The railway was opened in 1820 but closed before the turn of the century. In that time many buildings in London, the British Museum among them, were constructed of these blocks which arrived via the railway. It terminated at Teigngrace on the Stover Canal from where it was shipped to the Port of London. Branches of the granite track are seen around the tor; although the "rails" are not continuous, the track ran for over 13 km. Near the workings, some of the blocks have inscriptions of the initials of the men who laid them. Horses were used to pull lines of up to eight trucks and frequent team-changes were needed. The wheels ran along inward-facing flanges and hardly wore out; at the meeting of the various branch lines, points were operated in the same method as ironroads, by pulling rods to realign the rails. Hound Tor Coombe, in which the brook runs to the north, is another of the 'Gems' in Crossing's book. Arrive at this tor after visiting Haytor (q.v.)

HONEYBAG TOR   Widecombe   729787   445   M R
Chinkwell Tor 400 m S; Hameldown Tor 4 km NW; Easdon Tor 3 km NE; Hound Tor 1.5 km ENE; Haytor 3.25 km SE; Rippon Tor 3.5 km SSE; E. Webburn R. 700 m W.
The tallest pile is to the west of the summit, and there are many strangely shaped rocks among the piles. Approach from the cattle grid 2.5 km north of Widecombe. Go east uphill, through the gate then steeply east to the rocks on the horizon above you.

HOOKNEY TOR   Bovey   699812   497   M R
Hookner Tor [JC]
Hooknor Tor [SR]
Birch Tor 1.25 km WNW; Shapley Tor 1 km N; King Tor 1 km ENE; Hameldown Tor 850 m SSE; Grimslake to the S; W. Webburn 600 m W.
Access from Firth Bridge, below Grimspound, then north to the rocks or directly from the road due west of the tor 300 m away, if a parking spot is available.

HOUND TOR   Manaton   742790   414   M R
Great Hound Tor [EH]
Hayne Down 1.25 km N; Greator Rocks 650 m SE; Haytor 2.5 km SSW; Rippon Tor 3.5 km S; Honeybag Tor 1.5 km WSW; Hameldown Tor 4.25 km WNW; Becka Brook 1 km E.
Like Bellever and West Mill Tors, a wide area of turf seperates large outcrops forming an avenue; the area of rocks cover a wide amount of ground. Clitter lies on the north slope in abundance, though less so to the west from which direction you would proceed from the car park.
The celebrated mediaeval village is south-east of the tor; it was excavated in the early 1960s and Aileen Fox's book *Archaeology of South-West England* gives a more detailed account of the site. Proof has been found that the settlement was based on a Saxon domain. As the weather was similar to that we experience today, the wind and rain eventually damaged the wooden frame of the dwellings and the site was evacuated. The presence of stone was ignored by the 'villagers'; only the bases of walls remain, but they provide an insight into the shape and use of the buildings. Park at Swallerton Gate (GR 739792).

HOUND TOR   Taw   629890   495   K R
Houndetor [B] + [SR]
Hounteret [RISDON]
Hundatora [D]
Round Tor [EH]
Wild Tor 1.5 km SSW; Steeperton Tor 1 km WSW; Yes Tor 5 km WNW; Oke Tor 2 km NW; Buttern Tor 2.5 km ESE; Steeperton Brook 500 m W; Galleven Brook 700 m SW; Smallbrook 600 m N.
A tor with a flattish, grassy top, Hound Tor is only about 3 m high all round, but the site was even then considered prominent enough to be used as a landmark on the 1240 perambulation. To the north-east are Whitemoor Circle and Stone; the latter on the boundary between Lydford and Throwleigh parishes is also a perambulation 'marker'. To see the tor and the stones begin at South Zeal. Cross the former A30 and head towards Throwleigh, turn right at footpath sign to the moor heading roughly south-west. Beyond the enclosures, head for the more southerly of two trees which are near a triple stone row. Keep on this bearing and meet a slightly sunken track which you follow for another 3 km to the tor, passing the circle on your left with the stone 200 m beyond that.

HOUND TOR, LITTLE   Taw   631898   492
Steeperton Tor 1.75 km SW; Oke Tor 2 km W; Watern Tor 3 km S; Hound Tor 1 km SSW; Smallbrook 300 m W; Blackaton Brook 1 km NE.
This tor is hardly worth the name but consists of two large rocks over 2 m long and less than 1m high. They are found SW of the small cairn on the summit of the rise north of Whitemoor Circle. They face SW and can be seen from Hound Tor, from where you could visit the rocks.

HUCCABY TOR   Dart   657739   350   R
Huckaby Tor [SR]

R. Dart flows W–S 600 m away; Bellever Tor 3 km NNW; Combestone Tor 2.5 km SSE.

In the days when horse-racing was as prominent around the moor as it was in the more affluent areas of Britain, many local hunts and landowners set up a course on common lands within their own boundaries. Huccaby Tor was one such venue; the cropped grass was one advantage and the presence of good communications (even in those days) meant that the attendance was high. On 10 June 1909, King George V and Queen Mary watched racing here, an event to swell the crowds even more. The tor is reached from the gate to the west of Huccaby Cottage (GR 661736) walking 500 m NW passing Huccaby Ring on the way.

HUCKEN TOR   Walkham   548738   c.300   M R W
Okel Tor [C]

From this group of rocks it is difficult to see other tors clearly, especially in summer when vegetation is at its most luxuriant, or because the stacks are so spread out, but from the top of the most easterly, these are the figures: Vixen Tor 1 km NW; Feather Tor 1.5 km N of W; Pew Tor 1.75 km WSW; from the highest point, Little King Tor is 150 m NE; E Walkham 500 m W; Longash Brook 500 m N.

Many tors make up Hucken Tor, spread over 150 m from east–west downhill and each rocky pile is covered or surrounded by vegetation: grass on the granite along side patches of moss and lichens, and numerous dwarf oaks around and between the outcrops. A good place to visit if you're not in any hurry as, if it's hot, the trees will give shade enough, but it's not a tor for the claustrophobic to stay at for long.

HUNT TOR   Rattlebrook   557875   560   M R

Kitty Tor 1 km E; Higher Dunnagoat Tor 1 km S; Great Links Tor 1 km SW; Gren Tor 700 m NW; Sourton Tor 2.5 km NNW; Rattlebrook Head 250 m E; R. Lyd 1 km N and W.

Four main blocks stand either side of the packhorse track mentioned under Gren Tor, the predecessor of the railway to Rattlebrook peatworks, except this path leads to Kitty Tor. A pleasant spot to stop at on the way to other places. A start from Sourton, as for Gt Links Tor and others, will bring you to the turning circle on the railway track. Follow it south to Lydda Bridge, go up to Gren Tor and keep to the right-hand side of the track gradually ascending to Hunt Tor.

HUNTER'S TOR   Lustleigh   761824   c.130   R W

Sharpitor 1.5 km SE; Haytor 5.5 km S; Hayne Down 3 km SW; Easdon Tor 3 km W; Raven's Tor 600 m S but needs a steady descent from here; R. Bovey 700 m W and S, flows through Lustleigh Cleave, which is one "Gem" in the "Granite Setting" which Crossing describes.

The tor has the remains of fortifications around it, probably Iron-age, in the form of banks and ditches, but they are not so well defined as those at Cranbrook Castle above Fingle Bridge, but it is a fine position for warriors and present-day walkers alike. The latter group would find their way up to Hunters Tor via Sharpitor (q.v.), starting at Lustleigh, or from the lane near Barnecourt (GR 757832), going along the track south-east to Peck Farm, then using the signposts and yellow dots up to the tor which you can see from the lane.

HUNTER'S TOR   Teign   722898   c.180
Hunts Tor [C]

Meldon Hill 4.5 km SW; Kes Tor 6.5 km SW; Sharp Tor 800 m E (1 km by footpath); R. Teign steeply down 100 m to S and E.

Barely visible from Hunter's Path, the rocks are reached from the path below Castle Drogo (signposted from the road from Drewsteignton) below the point where the path makes a right-angle from north-west to north-east (or visit it after Sharp Tor).

INGRA TOR   Walkham   555721   339   Q R
Inga Tor [C]

Kings Tor 1.5 km N; North Hessary Tor 3 km NE; Leeden Tor 1 km ESE; Pew Tor less than 3 km NW; R Walkham 1 km W.

Approaching from the north or west, Ingra Tor prominently stands above the surrounding area, but it is met almost suddenly if a route from the south-east is chosen. Once in the vicinity, it is seen to be one high, conical mound with compact masses among patches of grass, quite an attractive tor by any standards. To the north, immediately below, runs the track of what was the Plymouth and Dartmoor railway, which was the idea of Sir Thomas Tyrwhitt. His plan was to establish a community on the moor which would centre on farming as a means of supporting the inhabitants. When that failed, granite-quarrying was suggested and a line from the waterside at Plymouth to the middle of the moor was laid. Many of the tors and outcrops on or close to the track were attacked and, like Ingra Tor, Kings Tor and Swell Tor were despoiled. The first tram (pulled by horses) ran in 1823 and the line as it existed, ceased to function in 1900. It was succeeded by the Princetown Line, a passenger train being the main user. Near this tor was a stopping-place where tourists could alight, go for a stroll and catch the train back to Plymouth, or wherever they wanted. Much of the original line was used by the later railway but, being able to make tighter turns, it cut off corners (see Yes Tor, a little to the east of Ingra Tor). The line finally closed down in 1956 not, as Hemery says, as a result of Dr Beeching – his axe fell in 1963 and after – he was not even connected with British Railways in '56, let alone chairman.

The easiest way to Ingra is from the lower car park on the B3212 below Sharpitor (q.v.) and walk 1.5 km NNW. The quarries are on the north-east slopes.

INGSTONE ROCK see Hingstone Rock

IVY TOR	Taw/Belstone	628936	c.250

No other tors are seen from this spot, being on a north-facing slope with the wooded valley of the Taw below, the gradient too steep behind it and far too low to glimpse any fellow tors. It lies on the edge of Skaigh Warren, a former supplier of rabbit meat to the tinners and local inhabitants of Sticklepath, South Zeal and other settlements.

Ivy Tor Mine (GR 627935 – south-west of the rocks) produced both arsenic and tin for a while. The simplest way to Ivy Tor is from Sticklepath. Take the road towards Skaigh, turning off after 300 m and walk alongside the Taw on its west bank. Keep in the same direction until the path dips down to the river, which is crossed by a wooden footbridge. Turn upstream, and make your way up the bank at an angle until you see the tor, in the trees 200 m from the bridge; it is 30 m from the R. Taw and the massive rocks are about 6 m tall on the north side.

KENT'S TOR	Tavy	517794	c.220	pt F W N

Kenter Tor [C]

Brimhill Tor 100 m NE; Fox Tor 500 m SW.

This, the fourth tor going north-east from Peter Tavy to Horndon Bridge, is made up of large blocks overlooking the R. Tavy to the south-east. It is itself south-east of Bennett's reservoir, adjacent to it. It holds water from the leats flowing from Wheal Jewel, issuing into the hydro-electricity station at Mary Tavy, the largest of its kind in England, and one of three connected with Dartmoor. Although on private land, it can be seen from the lane north-east of Cudlipptown.

KES TOR	Chagford/Teign	666862	437	R

Castor [SR]

Sometimes referred to as **Kestor Rock**.

Middle Tor 500 m SE; Watern Tor 3.75 km N of W; Rival Tor 3 km NW; Stonetor, just out of sight, 2 km WSE; Steeperton Tor 5 km NW; N. Teign 750 m NW; S Teign 1.25 km E.

A feature of the horizon when looking to the moor from the north and south, from many places on the north-east of the area. A lone, solid-looking tor with very little clitter, much grass and a rocky crown. The rock-basin on the summit once had a small rail around it to prevent sheep from falling in and drowning in the pool, which is often full. Kes Tor rises above a prehistoric field-system, probably Iron-age, to its north, the most interesting site of which is "Roundy-pound", a smithy kept apart from other dwellings by a wall seen on the side of the modern road to Batworthy. James Barber, in *Dartmoor – A New Study*, puts the date of this settlement at the fifth century BC.

Take the road out of Chagford to the north and bear left, signposted "Kestor". Continue following these signs until you enter the commons at the cattle-grid in 5 km. Go on to the end of the road, passing the pound to the right and stop where the road bends to cross the bridge to Batworthy. On the ground is room for half-a-dozen vehicles. Walk to the tor south east (400 m).

KING TOR   North Bovey   709815   470   R

Easdon Tor 2 km ENE; Hayne Down 3.5 km ESE; Hound Tor 4 km SE; Hookney Tor 1 km WSW; Shapley Tor 1 km WNW.

Tributaries of the R. Bovey run from the north to the north-west and on the east flowing north.

On the summit of the ground, a barrow is more prominent, the stones being visible before the tor comes into view to the north of the barrow. A visit to the tor is made from Firth Bridge, near which is a small parking area for sightseers going to Grimspound. Pass through the pound with the tors of Hameldown and Hookney to the right and left, respectively, and go to the summit of this ridge. Then walk 700 m NE to the barrow then to the tor.

KING TOR, LITTLE   Merrivale   551740   335   W

Gt Mis Tor 3 km NNE; Kings Tor 500 m ESE; Hucken Tor 150 km SW; Gt Staple Tor 2.25 km NNW; R. Walkham 900 m W; Longash Brook 400 m N.

From Four Winds, an excellent starting place to visit more than one tor, walk south towards King Tor, to reach the track of the Princetown Line and the Plymouth and Dartmoor railway, turn west. Where the two old tracks diverge, take the right-hand one, on nearly facing south while on this route, Little King Tor is immediately on the right of the track.

Mind how you go as damage to this wall is both unnecessary and illegal; a way around is found by going a few metres further on and doubling back. You also get a better view of the surrounding area as well as a different aspect of the rocks.

KING'S TOR   Merrivale   557738   c.385   M Q R
Great King Tor [EH]

Gt Mis Tor 3 km NNE; Swell Tor 600 m SSE; Little King's Tor 200 m WNW; Gt Staple Tor 2 km NNW; R. Walkham 1 km W.

The largest pile is on the summit and there's clitter to the north and west. The hill on which the tor stands is almost completely ringed by the track of the former Princetown Line. To the north-east, the earlier Plymouth and Dartmoor railway track takes a wider loop passing between the smaller tor of the same name and its big brother (see also Ingra Tor.) Being that bit higher than the point

where it crosses Yestor Brook, the track inclines before making the 180° sweep and as the trains slowed to breast the gradient, youths would jump off the train, scamper across 300 m of moor to re-alight as the train approached from the north, having travelled ten times as far as the boys in the same space of time.

The quarries are found to the south and south-west of the tor at ground level.

This tor, obvious from the starting point at Four Winds, east of Merrivale is reached by walking SSW for 1 km, but avoid miry ground away from the walls of Longash Farm's enclosures. (See Hucken Tor.)

KIT ROCKS   **East Dart**   **613827**   **520**   **M**
Kit Tor [c]
No other tors are visible from the rocks but Flat Tor is 1.25 km SSW; Fur Tor 2.5 km WNW; Sittaford Tor 2 km ENE; East Dart R. is to the west.
To find Kit Rocks, drive around Fernworthy Reservoir to the end of the road, park, walk NW through the gate and keep on this track until you emerge from the forest at GR 641844. Turn left and follow the worn path through two walls. At the second, where the Grey Wethers stone circles are, go uphill to Sittaford Tor. Walk SW to the ruin called Statt's House and then WNW for 1 km to the rocks. Statt's House was occupied by a peat-worker, so it is said. He (or she might have been a she) was probably not the gregarious type, didn't fall out with his neighbours and likely as not collected his own milk and newspapers.

KITTY TOR   **W. Okement**   **568872**   **578**   **H nrK P R**
Kit Tor [sr]
Green Tor 1.5 km SW; Gt Links Tor 1.75 km WSW; Hunt Tor 1 km WNW; Stenga Tor 600 m N; High Willhays 2.5 km NNE; Fur Tor 4.5 km SSE; W. Okement R. 1 km SE to NE; Rattlebrook 1 km W.
Relatively small outcrop but its position gives it prominence. A longer, lower pile is found near the flagpole. Come to the tor via Hunt Tor (q.v.).

KNATTBOROUGH TOR [starkey] Belstone   **611910**   **438**   **R**
Higher Tor 700 m NNE; Cosdon Beacon 2.5 km ENE; Hound Tor 2.5 km SSE; Oke Tor 1 km S; Yes Tor WSE; Winter 600 m N; R. Taw 700 m E; East Okement 450 m W.
To the right of the track from Belstone Moorgate (GR 617934) keeping roughly south, pass Winter Tor just off the track to your right after nearly 2 km then continue to the low-lying tor to the right of the path. Starkey's reference is the only one and he did not reveal his source.

LANGWORTHY TOR   **Widecombe**   **706772**   **409**   **R**
Chinkwell Tor 2.5 km NE; Hameldon Beacon 2.5 km N; Riddon Ridge 4 km WSW.
Exposed flat rock, flush with the turf, about 25 m long by 6 m wide with a 75 cm x 25 cm cuboid boulder at the eastern end. From the top of Church Lane from Widecombe, go through gate and follow the rough track as it bears to the right. Fork left on the gravel and near the top of the slope turn left to the tor in about 30 m.

LATCHELL TOR   **Manaton**   **757806**   **c.290**   **F N**
Lechole Tor
No other tors are visible, even in winter as this one is among thick vegetation. From the crossroads at Kes Tor Inn, go along the road to the east to the first track, turn left and at the next cross-track turn left and go along this for about 200 m. Turn left through the wood and bushes going uphill all the while. The tor is moss and lichen covered and extends for 30 m. Above the tor is Freeland Tower (GR 757809) which was used as a lookout post in WW2, but is now locked. From at least two angles, there are traces of steps from the tower. Not on access land, but permission could be obtained from local residents.

LAUGHTER TOR   **Dart**   **652757**   **420**   **M R**
Laugh Tor [donn:1765]
Lough Tor [c] + [eh]
Bellever Tor 1 km NW; Riddon Ridge 1.5 km NE; extensive views to the south over the West Dart valley and Holne Ridge, including S. Hessary Tor 6.5 km SW.

From the summit of the tor due south 300 m away is a standing stone, which may well have been erected at the same time as the stone row which is a little to the east. This is now dilapidated probably as a result of farmers wanting to build walls without too much effort, so using every available natural material. Many fields were enclosed as a result of the laws passed in the 1770s and several prehistoric sites were destroyed in this way. Of course, the National Park today would tell the vandal to replace every stone or face the consequences. Another interesting (well I think so) relic in the same vicinity is a rectangular wall of such a height that sheep would find it difficult to jump over(!) I thought at first that it was a sheep*fold* but, realising that it was so far away from the nearest farm at Dunnabridge, decided that it was a sheep*stell*. The shepherd knew how many animals were inside by jamming them all in. Goodness knows if he could work out the exact number if some heavily pregnant ewes were enclosed with some underfed tups. And what about those poor lambs which couldn't fit into the sheepstell? Did they go uncounted or did the shepherd fall asleep before he reached two hundred?

To get to Laughter Tor, enter the gate to the west of Huccaby Cottage, walk past Huccaby Tor, on the left, and continue in a north-westerly direction to the tor, or from Postbridge via Bellever Tor then through the gate between the two tors.

LE WEST SOLLE see Stenga Tor

LEATHER TOR   Walkham   563700   360   M R

Lether Tor [c] + [eh]. From the Celtic "llethr" = slope.
Sharpitor 400 m NW; Sheepstor due S across Burrator Reservoir; Down Tor 2 km ESE.

A good name for this tor especially the highest pile which is dramatically tall and craggy as well as steep. The rocks are particularly spectacular from the lakeside but easier to get to from the B3212. The outcrops are more or less aligned north-south and are lower towards the reservoir. A large amount of clitter needs to be negotiated if a climb to the top is undertaken from the south or east side. The track to the south which emerges from the woods to the east is the monk's path from Tavistock to Buckfast, not to be confused with the Abbots' Way. The path follows a series of crosses, many of which have been restored. There is one at the corner of the track (GR 561695)

and the road to Norsworthy Bridge; it is rather a slim version but if you imagine the area with no trees, even a cross so seemingly fragile as this would assume importance in foul weather.

The easy way to reach Leather Tor is from the car park on the B3212 below Sharpitor, pass that tor to the right and there in front of you is the tor, unless someone has moved it since the time of writing!

LEEDEN TOR   Meavy/Walkham   564718   389   M Q R
Leedon Tor [c] + [EH]
S. Hessary Tor 3.5 km E; Black Tor 1 km E; Hart Tor between those two; Gt Trowlesworthy 8 km SSE; King's Tor 2 km NNW; Staple Tor 4 km NNW; Cox Tor 5 km same direction; Roos Tor is to the right of Staple Tor; Gt Mis Tor 5 km N; Ingra Tor 1 km WNW; R. Meavy 1 km SE; Walkham Valley 2 km W.

The quarry is on the most easterly side of the five outcrops, which are scattered over 200 m. Approach from the road below Black Tor where a lay-by for two or three cars has been made. Leeden Tor is obvious due west. Between this tor and Ingra Tor, about 400 m from here, is a dry leat, the purpose of which is not clear, but it may have supplied water to the many small farms to the east of Walkhampton.

LEGIS TOR   Plym   571655   c.310   M
New Warren Tor [c] alternative name.
Leggis Tor [c]
Gutter Tor 1.5 km NNE; Hen Tor 2.5 km S of E; Gt Trowlesworthy Tor 1.5 km SSE; Shadyback Tor 750 m SSW.

One of the best examples of a vermin trap is found to the south of the main pile at the base. Many have viewed it, so there is a certain amount of erosion here. Rabbits were easy prey and the tinners, who liked a supply of fresh meat, relied on the warreners to supply them. The warreners devised a way of trapping vermin by causing them to run along a low wall until they entered the trap where a thin slab would be released behind the animal by its own movements. The dog would be sent in when the weasel or stoat was totally worn out in its efforts to escape. The area of short turf which extends over Ringmoor Down is now enclosed by a hideous fence (see Gutter Tor). Stiles on either side of Ringmoor Cottage allow access across Ringmoor Down to the tor, but it's best to keep to the line indicated by the signposts at the stiles. The tor is 1.5 km from the cottage.

LEIGH TOR   Dart   712715   150   R
Long Tor [c]
Aish Tor 1 km W but not visible; Poundsgate village 1 km NNW; R. Dart S and E.

A long and narrow tor, Leigh Tor runs from east to west covering over 80 m with some vegetation on its north face. The opposite face is nearly perpendicular in places and is used as a nursery slope for climbers. A stony track leads to the tor from near the top of Newbridge Hill.

LEIGHON TOR see Greator Rocks

LEIGHON TOR [c] + [EH]   Manaton   758787   c.350
Smallacombe Rocks (Grea Tor) 500 m SSW; Greator Rocks 1 km WSW; Hound Tor 1.5 km WNW; Becky Brook 500 m W.

Hemery's position of the tor (p. 64 *Walking the Dartmoor Railroads*) is out by 400 m. The map on the page shows the tor to be north-west of the summit of Black Hill, but nothing remotely like a tor is found there, not even a large boulder. The tor is topped by a pointed rock on the east side, and from here Hole Rock can be seen SSW. This rock is on the line of boundary stones (see Grea Tor) and a smaller stone stands below Hole Rock.

LETHER TOR see Leather Tor

LIDAFORD TOR see Littaford Tor

LIDFORD TOR see Lydford Tor

LINKS TOR, GREAT   Lyd   551867   586   M T
Lynx Tor [BG]
High Willhays 4 km NE; Kitty Tor 1.5 km ENE; Great Kneeset 3.75 km ESE; Fur Tor 5 km SE;

Brat Tor 1.75 km SW; Sourton Tor 3 km NNW; Rattlebrook 900 m E; R. Lyd 1.5 km N and W; Doe Tor Brook rises 700 m S.

One of the most prominent of all the tors, Gt Links is a landmark from much on the north-west moor. The tallest and highest pile is the westerly of the group and the smallest is conveniently the most easterly outcrop. Like Gren Tor, a vast expanse of country can be seen from the summit as far as Bodmin Moor and even towards the lower reaches of the R. Tamar.

| **LINKS TOR, LITTLE** | **Lyd** | **547870** | **510** | **R** |

Gt Links Tor 400 m SE; Arms Tor 1 km SW; Doe Tor 2 km SSW.

A single rock with lamellar bedding of granite. Access to this tor and to Gt Links Tor is from Sourton, as to Gren Tor (q.v.) but keep on the peat railway track until due north of Great Links, then contour around the small marsh at the head of Smallcombe. Little Links is to the right 300 m away.

| **LINTS TOR** | **W. Okement** | **580875** | **496** | **R** |

Lynch Tor [SR] which is confusing as the Lynch Tor we know lies above the east bank of the Tavy.

Dinger Tor 850 m NE; Gt Kneeset 2 km SSE; Fur Tor 4.5 km S; Kitty Tor 1.25 km W; Stenga Tor 1.25 km NW; Lints Tor Brook 150 m E and N; W. Okement 250 m W.

Another long rock running from north-west to south-east with the tallest part on the south-eastern end. Much of the Tor is partly grass covered; although not very tall, it is strikingly prominent from the Okement valley. This is the more interesting route to the tor: from the car park at Meldon Reservoir, cross the dam and go to the eastern end of the lake, then follow the river upstream for 3 km. Lints Tor is ahead, castle-shaped. You could follow the army track below High Willhays to Dinger Tor heading south all the time, but the going is tough on the feet!

| **LITTAFORD TORS** | **Dart** | **616772** | **466** | **R** |

Lidaford Tor [BG]

Longbetor [DONN'S MAP 1765]

Crockern Tor 1.25 km S. Beardown Tor 1 km WNW; Longaford Tor 900 m N; Bellever Tor 3 km ESE; W. Dart 500 m W; Cherrybrook 1.25 km E.

Lying above Wistman's Wood, a visit to the group of tors on this ridge, passing through the wood on the way back to Two Bridges, makes a fairly easy stroll. From the car park which is opposite the east entrance to the hotel parking area, go north through the gate, pass Crockern Farm on your left, go over two stiles before walking for 450 m NE to Littaford Tor.

(The map attributed to Donn shows the 'Dart' and 'W. Dart' having their confluence at Two Bridges, whereas it is the Cowsic which is the tributary of the W. Dart.)

| **LITTLE DOWN TOR** | **Deancombe** | **577694** | **340** | **R** |

205m W of Down Tor

LITTLE HISWORTHIE see Hessary Tor, South

| **LITTLE KNEESET** | **W. Okement** | **585842** | **507** | |

Grass on top of the rise, but a small stack of rock on the south slope just off the summit, amid a few scattered rocks, hardly worthy of being called clitter. Easy terrain for walking, though, compared to what is between this point and Great Kneeset, which is often marshy and uneven due to trial diggings by peat-workers over the years.

LITTLE PU TOR see Sampford Tor

LITTLE TOR   Okement   587907   525   **M R**

W Mill Tor 200 m N; Yes Tor 1 km SW; E Mill Tor 1.5 km SE; Belstone Tor 3 km NE.
As the name suggests, not a large tor. It could be said to be overshadowed by West Mill Tor, but this is impossible as Little Tor is to the south and can't possibly be in the shadow of its bigger neighbour.

LITTLE WHITE TOR   Peter Tavy   538787   420   **R**

Setters Tor 1 km SW; White Tor 250 m E.

LOGWELL ROCK   Dart   710734   250   pt **F W**

A craggy outcrop, 2 m high on the east side, on the river-facing gradient. Massive blocks with vegetation on and around the rock. It is 200 m W of Blackadon Tor, 400 m N of Leusdon Church.

LONG TOR see Leigh Tor

LONGAFORD TOR   E. Dart   616780   507   **R**
Southbeetor [DONN]

Higher White Tor 750 m NE; Bellever Tor 3.25 km ESE above the forest; North Hessary Tor 5.25 km SW; Gt Mis Tor 5.5 km WSW between Beardown and Lydford Tors; Rough Tor 2 km NW; East Dart 600 m W; Cherrybrook 1.25 km E.
The tor looks over Powder Mills to the south-east. This was the site of a gunpowder factory from 1844 to the late 1890s. The manufacture of an unusual commodity like gunpowder had to be undertaken away from centres of population and writers have told of the industrial history of the place. They have not mentioned the "Hairy Hands" legend at any great length though. Eden Phillpotts, the underrated author of many novels situated in and around Dartmoor, frequented the tor and one look at it will tell you why he so enjoyed both the tor and the panoramic views from its summit. The tor is almost a regular cone, with mosses and grass as much in evidence as the granite. A surprisingly little amount of clitter surrounds the mass and it would be easy to suppose that many of the walls in the area were in the 250 million BC part of the tor.
As with Littaford Tor, start from Two Bridges.

LONGASH TOR   Merrivale   551745   **N**

Not accessible, only visible from the stone row at Merrivale or from above from Kings Tor.

LONGBETOR see Littaford Tor

LONGTIMBER TOR   Peter Tavy   509783   150
Long Timber Tor [SR]

No other tors are visible, being on a flat piece of ground, but it is a fairly tall mass, rising up among oaks and beeches growing on all sides. It is the furthest south-west of those five between Peter Tavy and Horndon Bridge and is fenced off. It is alongside the footpath from Mary Tavy to its brother village. It is just south of the power station (see Kents Tor).

LOOK-OUT TOR see Hessary Tor, South

LOOKA TOR see Luckey Tor

LOUGH TOR see Laughter Tor

LOWER ARMS TOR   Lydford   541868   400

Arms Tor 500 m S; Gt Links Tor 1 km E.
A group of large rocks on the slopes of the Lyd Valley, which would be more spectacular if on a hilltop.

LOWERY TOR [C]   Burrator   557698   370

Found almost due south from the summit of Peek Hill and only 200 m off. On the 1906 OS map, 6 in:1 mile, but not appearing on the 1983 Leisure edition, Lowery Tor is one metre high on the north face but 6 m on the south; it is a single mass of compact blocks.
From the higher car park near Sharpitor, go 1 km due south over Peek Hill.

LOWTON TOR   Teign   667835   c.370   **F**
Loughten Tor

In Fernworthy Forest, so access is dependent of any forestry working going on at the time. From the main car park, go along the road to the west and turn left onto a track going uphill. In another 350 m or so, look to your left for the tor 200 m away. I found it immediately after an area of brush was cleared in early 2009. It is a relatively small area and only about 2 m high, but it's another tor to knock off your list!

LUCKEY TOR	**Dart**	**685720**	**200**	

Looka Tor [EH]
Lug Tor [C]
Sharp Tor 1 km N but not seen; Bench Tor 700 m ESE summit visible only from the top of the tor.
It almost rivals Vixen Tor in its height, but the setting of Luckey Tor is very different: trees and shrubs grow at the base of the face and the whole area abounds with deciduous woodland, and flat, grassy "lawns" between the tor and the Dart. Also the approach is completely opposite. Reaching these cliff-like formations, you start from the park at Dartmeet, cross the road and keep to a narrow worn path which soon enters the wooded banks of the river. Take care as, in places, the roots and the rocks mingle so when wet are hazardous. In 2.5 km, you find Luckey Tor on the left.

LULLINGYSSETE see Lynch Tor

LUR TOR See Broadown Tor (no one else can!)

LUXTON TOR	**Lee Moor**	**559633**	**300**	**R**

Sheepstor 5 km NNE; Sharpitor 7 km N; Trowlesworthy Tors 2 km NE; Shell Top 4 km E.
From the trig. pillar on Saddlesborough, go 50 m N to this low-lying rock group.

LYDFORD SHARP see Sharp Tor, Lyd

LYDFORD TOR	**Cowsic**	**600781**	**500**	**R**

Lidford Tor [SR]
Devils Tor 1.5 km N; Crow Tor 1 km NE; Higher White Tor 2 km ENE; North Hessary Tor 4.5 km SSW; Great Mis Tor 4 km WSW. W Dart R, E; Cowsic R, W.
Many of my companions have remarked on the fact that Lydford Tor is a long way from Lydford. So it is, but in days of old when Knights were bold, everyone walked or rode and this was one of their popular routes. The wall over which the stiles have been erected, is the northernmost border of Beardown Farm enclosures, and if you choose to walk the route from Two Bridges, seen later, one of these stiles will be of use. The Lich Way passes next to this tor, to the south. This was the way a mediaeval funeral procession would pass en route from the Dart valleys to Lydford. The parish had jurisdiction over most of the original Forest of Dartmoor. The burdensome journey was abandoned when Bishop Branscombe gave permission for inhabitants of Postbridge, Bellever and the hamlets in the East Dart area to go instead to Widecombe. The Bishop was an enthusiastic walker himself, as we know from the day that he left his loaf above Sourton... Now, each September, an overnight walk is undertaken by people who travel the length of the Lich Way and back to Lydford. The easiest route to the tor is from Holming Beam (see Conies Down Tor) whence a journey of 2 km NNE will bring you to the pile; a direct route like this one is often marshy in parts, but the going is relatively easy, once you have crossed the Cowsic. The West Dart is to the east.

LYNCH TOR see Lints Tor

LYNCH TOR	**Lyd/Tavy**	**565806**	**517**	**K P R**

Lullingyssete [B]
Fur Tor 3.5 km NE; Great Mis Tor 3.5 km S; White Tor 3 km SW; Hare Tor 4 km NNW; R. Walkham 800 m E; Baggator Brook 600 m N and W. Superb views across the Tavy and Tamar valleys.
(Actually, the highest rocks of the tor are a few metres from the line of perambulation, and the tor is slightly to the west of the higher ground. Also, the flagpole has been erected on Limsborough, the nearby cairn, but this too has been built out of one of the outcrops.)
A few score metres to the north will bring you to a depression running mainly from west to east (left to right) and is called "Black Lane". Many names connected with the peat industry include "black" and this track, like several on Dartmoor, was the route taken by trains of ponies laden with

peat from Walkham Head, where a wide area of ground was used for providing the fuel for the villages of Mary and Peter Tavy (not the couple who paid the earth for the peat, literally!). Much of the blackstuff was transported to Wheal Betsy and Wheal Friendship, mines in the area from which copper, arsenic and zinc were produced. Lynch Tor is reached from the gate at Wapsworthy (see Baggator), but stay on the track (the Lich Way) passing between two walls, used as a drift to control cattle and, keeping to the left-hand wall, ascend to the tor above you, with the flagpole as a guide. The rocks themselves are a few paces to the north-west.

LYNX TOR see Links Tor, Great

MAIDEN TOR [EH] Burrator 562681 290

Sheepstor 320 m N of E; Gutter Tor 2 km SE; Sharpitor 2.25 km N. Eric Hemery, in Walking Dartmoor's Waterways, *p. 12 refers to this tor on Sheepstor's western slope, fairly near the bottom of the hill.*

It is seen to be three piles descending westwards, quite tall as outcrops go, but as on a low altitude, not as impressive as other tors of similar dimensions. The tor is found 130 m from the drift lane off the road running round Burrator Reservoir (GR 560683).

MANATON ROCKS Manaton 748816 c.33 M R
Manaton Tor [C IN 'GEMS']

Hunters Tor (Lustleigh) 1.5 km NE; Haytor 4.5 km E of S; Hayne Down 1.5 km SW with Hound Tor behind; Easdon Tor 2 km WNW; R. Bovey 1 km NE.

Take footpath going north from the village church (on the west side) and arrive at the top in 300 m.

MANGA ROCK Teign 636858 450 K

Probably the smallest item on this list, but quite an important little article as far as bound-beaters are concerned. It is barely visible from a distance, but it is the largest rock in the vicinity. The "G" inscribed stands for Gidleigh, being on the parish boundary as well as a perambulation mark.

MEL TOR Dart 693726 346 M R
Mil Tor [C]

Rippon Tor 5.5 km NE; Saddle Tor 6.5 km NE; Aish Tor 1.5 km SE; Bench Tor, across the Dart, 800m S; Luckey Tor 1 km SW; Combestone Tor 2.5 km WSW; Sharp Tor 1 km NW; Yar Tor 2 km NW; also Buckland Beacon is 4 km E.

From the west this group of large rock-piles appears to be one continuous mass with no gaps between the stacks. A superb outlook in most directions, it's a fine collection of rocks. On top of the highest mass is a good example of a rock basin. From Bel Tor Corner, follow Dr Blackall's Drive around the zig-zags and Mel Tor appears ahead after 250 m.

MELDON HILL   Chagford   696861   390   M R T

A prominent hill from the south of the town; from the west, several main groups of rocks are clearly seen. The most interesting fact about this hill is that Chagford Golf Course was situated on its slopes. Mr Webber, a trader in Chagford, possesses a sign naming it.

MIDDLE TOR   Teign   669858   c.430   R

Frenchbeer Rock 500 m SE; Thornworthy Tor 800 m SSW; Wild Tor 5 km WNW; Hound Tor 5 km NW; Kes Tor 500 m NW; Meldon Tor 3 km E; S. Teign 500 m SE.

A single mass of rock on short turf, with a prominent rocky "lump" on the west. From Batworthy (see Kes Tor) go to Kes Tor and go a further 500 m SE.

MIDDLEWORTH TOR   Deancombe   575672   c.380   F

Down Tor 600 m NE; Sheepstor 1 km SW.

From Norsworthy Bridge, at the east end of Burrator Reservoir, follow the track going south at first. In 400 m the ruins of Middleworth Farm appear on the right. The tor is in a scrubby area to the left and about 100 m from the track. The farm was one of nine abandoned when the reservoir was constructed in 1897 and enlarged 20 years later

MIL TOR see Mel Tor

MILL TOR, EAST   Taw   600899   513   H M R
East Mil [C]

Oke Tor 1.25 km ENE; Steeperton Tor 2.25 km SE; Gt Links Tor 6 km SW; Yes Tor 2 km N of W; West Mill Tor 1.5 km NW; Belstone Tor 2.5 km NNE; E. Okement R. 600 m E; Blackaven Brook 300 m W.

Many scattered piles and rock masses covering over 300 m north to south, the summit (from which these directions are taken) being on the second main pile from the south. Easy to find: on the 'ring road', stop at New Bridge (GR 596903) and walk uphill to the east.

MILL TOR, WEST   W. Okement   588910   541   K M R
West Mil [C] + [EH]

East Mill Tor 1.5 km SE; Yes Tor 1 km SW; Sourton Tors 4.5 km WSW; Oke Tor 2.5 km ESE; Moor Brook 400 m E; Redaven Brook 600 m SW and W; Blackaven Brook 1 km SE.

A popular site for rock-climbers, particularly the southern face of the most southerly outcrop. This rock overlooks the line of the perambulation, from Yes Tor to Cullever Steps. The higher piles form an avenue, the granite having broken away from the bulk of the tor and fallen down the slopes to lie as clitter. Grass readily grows among the blocks and the tor is frequented by sheep and cattle. Access to West Mill Tor is from the the military road. Either stop below Row Tor and head uphill past those rocks to this tor which is 1 km further or, if you have a four-wheel drive, a risky climb on the stony track in the same direction will bring you under West Mill.

MIS TOR, GREAT   Walkham   562769   538   H K P R
Misor [BA] who names the tor after the god of heather!
Mistorr [SR]
Mystor [B] + [RISDON]

Fur Tor 6.5 km NNE; N. Hessary Tor 3 km SE; King's Tor 3 km almost S; Gt Staple Tor 2 km SW; Roos Tor 1.75 km S of W; White Tor 2.5 km NW; Hare Tor over 7 km NNW; Gt Links Tor 10 km W of N; Lynch Tor 3.5 km N; R. Walkham 1 km W; Blackabrook 1.25 km E flowing S.

A little to the north of the flagpole is an example of a rock-basin where a stone, lodged in a crack in the rock has, over the centuries, eroded a circular area about 600 cm across and up to 20 cm deep. It's got a break in the wall, as if to let any excess water out and the name "Mistor Pan" is written into some accounts of the definition of the forest perambulation. There is some debate as to whether the "pan" is the heath to the north-east of the tor, but logic should prevail and what looks like a pan is therefore called à pan. It was there when the Knights did the rounds. From Rundlestone Corner, go between the walls NNW for 2 km on the track; it is in sight all the way.

MIS TOR, LITTLE **Walkham** 564764 480 **K R**
Wain Tor [c]
Dominated by Gt Mis Tor 600 m uphill, other tors are recognised and have been listed under "Big Brother" (or sister, if it's Mis!) Roos Tor is now 2 km due west and Gt Staple Tor 2 km S of W; New Forest corner is marked by a small stone with DCP (Directors of Convict Prisons) to the east.
Many traces of settlements, banked earth in the main, lie west of the mass and further downhill, on the bank of the river are good examples of blowing houses, both with mortar and mould-stones. In 1987, stiles were erected giving permitted access to Merrivale Newtake and it is good manners to use them when crossing the enclosure. On the tor itself is a crude memorial replacing the one which was fixed, proof shown by four holes on the south-facing wall of the rock. You pass Little Mis Tor on the way to Gt Mis Tor (which is convenient!)

NARROW TOR **Sheepstor** 566686 c.320
Narrator as in Plantation
Lether Tor 2 km N; Down Tor 2 km NE; Eylesbarrow 3 km E.
There are two or three prominent stacks on the north side of Sheepstor. Narrow Tor is exactly that, narrow but with a cleft and is the largest of the three piles.

NAT TOR **Sheepstor** 571673 323 **E W**
Gutter Tor 700 m SE; Sheepstor 1 km NW.
Not accessible, although 100 m from Burcombe Lane from Sheepstor Village to the Scout Hut. The small pile faces Sheepstor Brook and the tor of the same name. The tor is less than 4 m high and 6 m wide.

NAT TOR **Tavy** 545824 340 **R**
White Tor 3.5 km S; Brent Tor 7.5 km WSW.
R. Tavy flows from NE to SW; 'flows' is an arbitrary word for in normal conditions, the river is the second-fastest running in the British Isles, only the Tay in Scotland being quicker. By parking at Lane End, walking 1 km E and stopping on the rocks, you will have reached Nat Tor. Reddaford Leat is crossed on the way (see Ger Tor).

NATTADON TOR **Chagford** 705866 323
Nat Tor Down [c]
Meldon Tor (Hill) 1 km SW; Beetor 2.5 km S; Kes Tor 4 km W.
The main rock pile is on the north-west slope and is visible from the road to the west. An Iron-age fort was probably situated on the top of the hill. To get to the top of the hill, take the road south from Chagford Square (New St) then turn left in 500 m. A footpath leads off to the left, this road between houses. Go uphill to meet the tor before reaching the summit. Alternatively, drive from Chagford on the Moretonhampstead road for 1200 m to where the common land meets the road. A footpath signpost on the right tells you you're nearly there.

NEW WARREN TOR see Legis Tor

OKE TOR **Taw** 612900 456 **H M R**
Oak Tor [D. BRUNSDEN & J. GERRARD IN *DARTMOOR, A NEW STUDY*]
Ock Tor [C, IN 'GEMS']
Belstone Tor 2 km N; Hound Tor 2 km SE; Gt Links Tor 7 km SW; Steeperton Tor 1.5 km SSE; Yes Tor 3 km W; West Mill Tor 2.5 km WNW; R. Tae 750 m SE to NE; E Okement 600 m SW to NW.
A prominent group of granite outcrops which runs north-south along the same ridge as the Belstone range of tors. Oke Tor is an example of both vertical and horizontal bedding of the rock, forming irregular-sized blocks but with a uniform shape. Close to the tor is a shed-like structure which was used by the army as a stable, but nowadays by walkers as a convenience. Surely, a concealed or unobtrusive tree or rock would suffice and what is left behind would disintegrate biologically in the open air: so would the stench. By the way, Hangingstone Hill was equally misused in this way. Approach Oke Tor from Belstone Moorgate, keeping on the track for 3.5 km almost due south.

OKEL TOR see Hucken Tor

OLD HOUSE ROCKS   Widecombe   715787   487

Honeybag Tor 1.25 km E; Chinkwell Tor 1.5 km SE; Hayne Down 3 km NE.
Nearby is a boundary stone inscribed with 'Old House' one of many on Hameldown Ridge showing the extent of the former Duke of Somerset's manor of Natsworthy.

OTTERY TOR   Belstone/Taw   625924
Lady Brook Tor

Steeperton Tor 2.5 km S; Oke Tor 2.5 km SSW; Belstone Tor 1 km W; R. Taw 200 m W; Ivy Tor Water 300 m E and N.
Consisting of large blocks the tor, which is not named on OS maps, has a maximum height of 6 m and covers no more than 20 m E-W. Extensive but low clitter covers the slope towards the Taw. The outcrop is best seen from the path that passes Bernard's Acre south of the village and from whose occasional residents the name was forthcoming. To stand on the rocks, walk from the car park, through the village bearing left at the Green then, opposite 'The Tors', turn eastwards downhill on the track to the footbridge over the Taw. Cross it and make height as soon as possible to avoid the marshy ground, but bear right at the top of the wall of Skaigh Warren. Walk about one kilometre SSE; the tor shows against the skyline before very long, but make sure you don't drop down too much, especially after negotiating Tor Water.

OUTCOMBE ROCKS see Click Tor

OVALS TOR see Holwell Tor

OVER TOR [c]   Walkham   558753   380

Eric Hemery refers to "Over Tor Gert" to the north of the rock, as well as to the tor itself. King's Tor 1.5 km S; Hollow Tor 1.5 km ESE.
From Four Winds, on the B3212, walk 300 m NW to the tor; the large rock which is less than 100 m further north is Church Rock. To the west are the remains of Merrivale Warren, another rabbit-breeding centre of days past. (See Legis Tor and Sharp Tor as other warren sites.)

OXEN TOR see Cadworthy Tor

PEEK HILL   Burrator   557699   400   R
Peak Hill [c] + [EH]

West from Sharpitor, this height has a few low-lying slabs and further small groups of rocks protrude from the even line of gradient all around with more on the south side, overlooking Burrator. Cement bases show the position of a radio mast which stood here until the mid-1970s.

PEN BEACON   Cornwood   599629   427   R T

A prominent height, surmounted by a cairn and a trig. point, one kilometre south of Shell Top, but visited only after a steep climb from East Rook Gate; a much easier route from the north or east may be preferable. Seen from the A38 either side of Ivybridge, Pen (sometimes Penn) Beacon rises above another of the by now famous 'Gems', Hawns and Dendles which is an area of woodland on the west bank of the R. Yealm and is a National Nature Reserve. It was named after two former owners of separate woods, the division between them now almost obliterated under vegetation. Pen is a Celtic word which means "hill".

PENSHIEL see Shell Tor

PEPPERDON ROCKS   M'hampstead   777854   357   R

Blackingstone Road 500 m NE; Mardon Down 2.5 km NW.
A group of large rocks on the hillside.

PEW TOR   Walkham   532735   305
Pu Tor [c] + [EH]

Gt Staple Tor 2.5 km NNE; Vixen Tor 1.25 km NE; King's Tor 2.25 km E; Cox Tor 3 km N.
This tor is worth a visit. It is a good example of an avenue tor as is Bellever and West Mill Tors; a veritable lawn among the piles! The amount of quarrying undertaken in this area has left few remains of iron or any faint trackways, but there are clearly defined faces which were produced

by man's efforts rather than those of nature. Along the south slopes can be seen small, dressed stones, less than a metre high, inscribed "SSP" – Sampford Spiney Parish. On the most northerly of the piles is a rock-basin, a depression formed by a small stone being rubbed by wind or water in a groove, enlarging it by attrition until a cup- or saucer-shaped dip is produced over thousands of years. The valley of the R. Walkham to the east is yet another spot considered by William Crossing to be a 'Gem'. Access to Pew Tor takes very little effort (true!). Go south from Pork Hill car park 1.5 km, passing Feather Tor, crossing the Grimstone and Sortridge Leat and the old quarries (on your right) before reaching the rocks.

PIL TOR   Widecombe   735759   420   M R
Top Tor 300 m NNE; Saddle Tor 1.5 km NE; Rippon Tor 1 km E; Wind Tor 3 km W.
Blackslade Mire to the south-east prevents any approach from that direction in anything but dry weather. The bog forms the headsprings of Blackslade Water which eventually runs south-west. Another avenue tor, large piles of granite, good views all round. Widecombe Church can be seen in the valley to the north-west and, if you're longsighted, you may depict the line of boundary-stones in the marsh to the east and south-east. At Hemsworthy Gate, from where you can visit the tor, there is a stone set into the wall at the concave right-angle south of the road junction. It bears a cross and is the first of a straight line of stones which runs SSW along the marsh. They mark the parish boundary between Widecombe to the west and Ilsington and Ashburton to the east. From Hemsworthy Gate, walk 700 m south of west to some well-defined banks. They are presumed to be prehistoric enclosures, the more usual form being a circular pound with hut circles within. These banks make rectangles, but there are still Iron-age type dwellings within many of them. Pil Tor lies directly west, a gentle enough gradient to climb.

PIN TOR   Teign   756887   323   R
Hay Tor 12 km S; Mardon Down 1.5 km SW.
East of Willingstone Rock, with access from a gate on the north side of the road from Cranbrook Castle to Clifford Bridge.

PROWTYTOWN ROCKS [EH] Tavistock   528745   300
This area can easily be missed by visitors approaching from Pork Hill car park as, looking from the north, little suggests that a wall of rock is near by. As the cliffs face south-west, try walking to Windy Post (see Feather Tor), go north-west aiming towards the enclosure wall forming a right-angle, 300 m away, then, keeping close to the wall, without descending too much, look north to the clear line of rocky cliffs.

PU TOR see Pew Tor

PUGGIESTONE [SR]   Chagford   687876
On private land between Leigh Bridge and Holystreet Manor, on the north of the road. The rock is in the grounds of the house named after the outcrop.

PUPERS ROCK   W. Wallabrook   672674   467   M R
Puppers Rock [SR]
Two piles of granite form Pupers: one is called Inner Pupers, can you guess what the other's called? A small pointed cairn is on the summit of Inner Pupers, the stack nearer to Ludgate, where it is possible to leave one or two cars with care (i.e. before you get to Hayford House on the lane from Cross Furzes). The piles are on an ancient reave which can be traced from near Harbourne Head to the south (GR sq. 6965) to the summit of Snowdon (668684).

RABBIT TOR   Swincombe   634698   c.400
Fox Tor 0.5 km E; S Hessary Tor 4.5 km NW; Bellever Tor 6.5 km N; Sharp Tor 6 km NE.
Two larger piles, 2.5 m high and 100 m above a scattering of large boulders.

RAVEN ROCK   Dart   730715   150
Unfortunately, this is in **private woodlands**.

RAVEN'S TOR   Lustleigh   762819   c.250   M
Hunters Tor 600 m N; Manaton Tor (Rocks) 1.5 km WSW; R. Bovey to the W and S.
Two possible routes are suggested to reach this tor. From Manaton, take the footpath to Horsham, which is roughly due east, go downhill to cross the Bovey then go steeply uphill north-east, walking ahead at the T-junction of paths. Or, if you begin at Lustleigh, 2 km away, take the road towards Moretonhampstead. After nearly 1 km, a steep climb is met with a lane coming from the left. Continue for another 200 m, then take the footpath to the left, staying on a westerly bearing to meet Sharpitor. Go NW passing Harton Chest, a large cuboid of granite on your left, then a further 450 m NNW downhill will bring you to Raven's Tor.

RAVENS' TOR   Lydford   504840   c.170   E
On National Trust land above the west bank of the Lyd in Lydford Gorge. On the map, a woodland track is shown which runs close to the tor, but this is fenced in and not accessible to the public. The paths in the gorge itself are open, but an admission charge must be paid to visit the valley; it is, as you would expect, yet another of William Crossing's 'Gems in a Granite Setting'!

RIPPATOR see Rival Tor

RIPPER TOR see Rival Tor

RIPPON TOR   Haytor   747756   473   R T
Rippin Tor [J] According to him the next highest point on the moor after Cosdon! But he was writing in 1823, before his theodolite had arrived from the mail order firm.

Rippen Tor [EH]

Saddle Tor 1 km NE; Haytor to the right of Saddle; Bag Tor 1.5 km E; Buckland Beacon 2.5 km SSW; Pil Tor 1 km WNW; Source of R. Sig due E; Source of Blackslade Water 1 km W.

The summit of Rippon Tor is a mass of loose stones and remains of cairns. An incised cross is on a slab of granite near to topmost point and there is a small outcrop 30 m to the east of the trig. point. From the higher car park below Haytor Rocks, walk south-west and follow the wall around to go south towards the small gate in the wall ahead of you. An alternative way is to leave the car on the Ashburton road from Hemsworthy Gate (the first junction after Haytor) and pass through the gate which is due west of the tor.

RIVAL TOR   Wallabrook   643881   421   R
Rippator [OS]
Ripper Tor [EH]

Kes Tor 3 km SE; Watern Tor 2 km SW; Wild Tor 2 km WSW; Hound Tor 1.75 km NW; Gallaven Brook 300 m W and S; Teign 1.5 km S.

Visit Rival Tor from Buttern Tor (q.v.) which is 1 km NE of this tor. It is difficult to approach from any angle especially after prolonged rain.

ROBOROUGH ROCK   Yelverton   515672   c.190
Udal Tor [RW]
Ullestor [C]
Yelverton Rock [EH ON HIS MAP]

Cox Tor 9 km NNE with Gt Staple Tor to its right the same distance away; North Hessary Tor 9.5 km NE; Sheepstor 5 km ENE.

One long mass of rock on level ground, this tor is on the edge of the National Park. It is not very difficult to find... park next to it! It is 1 km from Yelverton roundabout on the A386 Plymouth Road. On the OS map 6 in:1 mile, a house situated 140 m NW of the rock is named Udal Torre, but the rock itself is called Roborough.

ROLLS TOR see Roos Tor

ROOK TOR   Lee Moor   602617   290

No major pile, but large scattered boulders. Find the tor from East Rook Gate which is about 300 m to the east of Rook Tor.

ROOS TOR   Walkham   543766   454   P R

Rolls Tor [c] + [jc] + [sr]
Roose Tor [c]

Staple Tor 600 m S; Gt Mis Tor 2 km N of E; White Tor 2.25 km N; Fur Tor 8 km NE; R. Walkham 1 km E; Grimstone and Sortridge Leat begins on the Walkham to the north-east and flows south to beyond Staple Tor on the west bank of the river.

Another of the fascinating items around this part of the moor is the circle of standing stones, not of the prehistoric age but erected by the Duke of Bedford (not personally) to maintain a steady supply of granite thus preventing other quarrymen taking stone from what the Duke claimed was his. Under whose authority the claim was made had not been established, but nowadays few souvenir hunters bother to pick up chunks of rock; they can though, recognise the stones by the capital 'B' and close by, a crossed 'O' inscribed on a flat stone. Arrive at this tor by way of Pork Hill car park, 1.5 km N to the top of Cox Tor, then the same distance NE to Roos Tor.

ROUGH TOR	**Dart**	**606798**	**548**	**H P R**

Row Tor [c]

Crow Tor 1 km S; N. Hessary Tor 6.25 km SSW; Devils Tor 1 km WSW; Fur Tor 3.75 km NNW; Sittaford Tor 4.25 km NE; Lower White Tor 1.25 km ESE; West Dart 500 m flowing from NE to SE; Cowsic 1.25 km W; Summer Brook 300 m N.

Viewed from many angles, the tor is shaped like a submarine so it is easily recognisable, but only if you remember the name (!). Access to Rough Tor: as to Crow Tor then due north.

ROUGH TOR [c]	**Burrator**	**576684**		**E**

Marked as being in Roughtor Plantation on OS maps as far back as the 1906 edition. Its most probable location is at a point 350 m W of an old-type stile and 35 m above a vehicle track, 10 m above a terraced path in the forest. There is a mass of moss covered rocks up to 5 m high.

ROUND TOR see Hound Tor, Taw

ROW TOR	**Dart**	**623801**	**c.510**	**M R**

Lower White Tor 1km SSW; Rough Tor 1.5km W; Hartland Tor 2km E.

A visit to these rocks from Lower White Tor will take you across the head of Cherrybrook at Hollowcombe Bottom, but there are worse climbs on the moor! The wall around Archerton newtake will act as a guide.

ROW TOR	**Okehampton**	**593916**	**468**	**M P R nr K**

Rough [sr]

West Mill Tor 800 m SSW; Yes Tor 2 km WSW; Belstone Tor 2 km N of E; Winter Tor 1.75 km E; Oke Tor 2.5 km SE; Blackaven Brook 800 m E; Moor Brook 500 m W.

ROWDON ROCK	**Bridford**	**812860**		**X**

Close to footpath from the village to Laployd Barton.

ROWDEN TOR [c]	**Widecombe**	**698761**	**356**	**R**

Wind Tor 1 km ESE; Corndon Tor 2 km SW; West Webburn 1 km SW.

The tor is not over 3 m high, if that. The single pile is flat and, like Wind Tor, grassy on top. Park at the old quarry at 701761 and go WSW uphill.

RUGGLESTONE ROCK	**Widecombe**	**727764**	**290**	**N**

We are talking of the granite block here, not the pub of the same name. A massive (by any Dartmoor standards) rock above the road behind the pub had a logging-stone look to it. That is, you might have been able to rock the rock if your visit to the Inn had been worthwhile. On the slope of the hill on which Hollow Tor stands, the rock is surrounded by walls, on **private land**.

RUNDLESTONE TOR	**Princetown**	**576746**	**c.590**	**K M**

N. Hessary Tor 500 m ESE; Hollow Tor 500 m W; Gt Mis Tor 2.5 km NW.

At the head of Longash Brook is beyond the road to the N and W. The name may derive from "roundle" = of or about a rock-basin, of which there is an example on the largest pile. From Rundlestone Corner (at the phone box on the B3357) walk up the road towards the mast for 300 m then turn right at the wall corner to the tor.

SADDLE TOR — Haytor — 750764 — 428 — **M R**

Haytor 1.25 km NE; Bag Tor 1.5 km SE; Rippon Tor 1 km SW; Holwell Tor 1.25 km N; Becky Brook 800 m W.

Appropriate name when seen from the east or west. Park beneath the tor on the Bovey to Widecombe road beyond the top car park under Haytor.

SADDLESBOROUGH — Lee Moor — 559632 — 303 — **R T**

Made up of large outcrops, which are not so tall on the northern side, this tree-accompanied group lies to the north-west of the summit. Quite an attractive spot in itself, although it has the china-clay works sprawling over the terrain on one half of the panorama. To the west and south, views of the Plym valley are extensive, as well as some of the tors of south-west Dartmoor. At present the rocks are not in the National Park

SAMPFORD TOR [C] — Walkham — 531732 — c.290 — **Q R**
Little Pu Tor [EH]

From Pew Tor 200 m SSW.

The small pile is among scattered hawthorns and rowans. Approach from Oakley Cottage on the Moortown road then go 500 m E.

SANDY HOLE ROCKS — Dart — 623813(S) 620816(N) — 490–500

From Postbridge, follow the R. Dart upriver on the west bank (well worn for the first 600 m) for 2.5 km to Dart Turn, then keep on the same bank for a further 2 km, passing the picturesque waterfall on the way. The southernmost group is seen to the left of the path just before the narrow part of the pass, while the other group is nearly 300 m further on, on the same side. Sandy Hole Pass is the name given to the narrowing of the river to facilitate the extraction of tin ore in Tudor times and later.

SCABTORA see Scobitor

SCAREY TOR — E. Okement/Belstone — 606924 — 365 — **R**
Skir Tor [C]

Belstone Tor 800 m SE; Winter Tor 1 km SSE; Row Tor 1.5 km SW.

E. Okement flows from the S-W-N passing within 100 m of the tor. Clitter below the tor extends almost to the river. Some trees among rocks; from Belstone Moorgate, follow track SW to an angle in the wall, then walk 1 km SSW to the tor.

SCATTER ROCK — Teign — 821854 — 289 — **N Q X**

This is a former quarry for basalt. Crossing calls it Skat.

SCOBITOR — Widecombe — 723750 — 300 — **E W**
Scobetor Rocks [C]
Scabtora [D]

E. Webburn 1 km W.

A track leads to the farm road from between Cold East Cross and Widecombe, but no public access is allowed.

SCORHILL TOR — Teign — 659872 — c.380 — **R**

Kes Tor 1 km SSE; Rival Tor 2 km NW,1; Watern Tor 3 km S of W; R. Teign 150 m S.

A small outcrop of large flattish stones and clitter. Scorhill Circle is 600 m NW. Approach from Berrydown, following the wall to the south 500 m after corner.

SETTERS TOR — Peter Tavy — 532779 — 360 — **M**

White Tor 1.5 km NE; Gt Mis Tor 3 km ESE; Roos Tor 2 km SE; Cox Tor 2 km S.

Follow the track from the quarry above Peter Tavy, passing Boulters Tor on your left. Pass between walls and just beyond the last corner of the right-hand wall Setters Tor is seen ahead and to the right of the track. It is made up of several small piles up to 3 m high.

SHADYBACK TOR [C] — Plym — 567649 — 250
Shearaback [C]

Legis Tor 750 m NNE; R. Plym to N and W.
The tor is situated 300 m N of Trowlesworthy Warren House, close to the Plym. It is another one of those within National Trust area.

SHAPLEY TOR **North Bovey** **699821** **+460** **R**
King Tor 1 km ESE; Hookney Tor 1 km S; Birch Tor 1.25 km WSW; Easdon Tor 3 km E; E. Bovey River 600 m NW; Coombe Brook 700 m E.
Access: from Moorgate car park (GR 698834) walk south for 1.25 km to tor.

SHAPTOR ROCK **Bovey Tracey** **809808** **240** **R X**
Sharptor Rock [EH]
Within a few hundred metres of a disused mine at GR 806810, 1 km W of Higher Bowden north of footpath through wood.

SHARP TOR **Dartmeet** **687729** **370** **R**
Yar Tor 1.25 km NW; Corndon Tor 1.25 km N; Bench Tor 1.5 km SSE; Mel Tor 1 km SE; R. Dart 700 m S; Rowbrook 300 m W; Simonslake 400 m E; Venford Reservoir due S 2 km away.
Another aptly named tor, appearing sharp from the north. One km to the south-west are the remains of Vaghill Warren. Sharp Tor can be reached from the parking space at the top of Dartmeet Hill on the Ashburton–Two Bridges road: go 500 m S, or walk 1 km W from Bel Tor Corner (GR 695731).

SHARP TOR **Erme** **649617** **414** **R**
Three Barrows (Tor) 1 km NNE; Wacka Tor 1.5 km ENE; Butterdon 3 km SSE; Stalldon Barrow 1.25 km NW; R. Erme 500 m W below a steep slope, at the bottom of which is Piles Copse, one of three ancient woods on the moor, but the height of these oaks far exceed those in Wistman's Wood and are on average taller than the trees in Blacktor Copse.
A ruined cairn lies to the north-east of the tor. Just below the rocks is the concrete pipeline used at the beginning of the 20th century to take china clay suspended in water from Redlake to the north, to the railway near Bittaford to the south. Most of the heavier material and equipment was transported by the railway 300 m to the east. Although it can be hard on the feet, the track provides an easy route to the remote parts of the southern moor.
The car park at Harford Moorgate (GR 643596) is the best starting point to visit the tor and Piles Copse.

SHARP TOR **Lyd** **550849** **519** **M R**
Lydford Sharp [EH]
Hare Tor 700 m S; Lt Hare Tor 800 m SW; Brentor 9 km WSW; Brat Tor 1.25 km NW; Arms Tor 1.75 km NNW; Gt Links Tor 2 km N; Chat Tor 600 m NE; Doe Tor Brook 1 km N; Wallabrook 800 m WSW.
Mostly of large blocks; fine scenery over the Lyd Valley to the west. Approach the tor from High Down (see Arms Tor), reach the Lyd and bear south, crossing the river when possible. Doe Tor comes into sight shortly above and on the other side of the Doe Tor Brook. Walk to the tor then go 1 km E across clitter with care up to Sharp Tor. Alternatively, start from Lane End (see Ger Tor and others) and include this tor in a round trip to Tavy Cleave and Hare Tor.

SHARP TOR [C] **Peter Tavy** **525771** **340** **R**
Great Combe Tor 300 m NW; Boulters Tor 1 km N; White Tor 2.5 km NE; Roos Tor 2 km ESE; Cox Tor 1 km ESE. On a path from Peter Tavy to Merrivale, a semi-circular cliff facing north 18 m high. Access from Pork Hill via Cox Tor.

SHARP TOR [C] **Tavy Cleave** **554832** **420** **R**
Tavy Cleave Sharp [EH]
Hare Tor 1 km N; Ger Tor 800 m W; Fur Tor 3.25 km E; R. Tavy (of course) below to the east and south.
Sharp Tor is the highest and largest of the five rockpiles which constitute Tavy Cleave Tors. Probably the easiest way to this tor is to go to Hare Tor (q.v.) and then south to Sharp Tor.

SHARP TOR	Teign	729899	210	

Overlooking the precipitous slope of the Teign above Fingle Gorge, the tor is of shale, not granite. Hunters Tor is 1 km W along the footpath (Hunters Path); opposite is Cranbrook Castle above the woods. From Drewsteignton, take the Two Moors Way going south for 1 km to meet the path, turn right; Sharp Tor is 200 m away. To the left (east) along Hunters Path the way drops down to Fingle Bridge, another of William Crossing's 'Gems'.

SHARP TOR [c]	Widecombe	729780	430	R

Hollow Tor 1.75 km S; Bonehill Rocks 600 m SSE; E. Webburn 800 m W.

This tor is found half way between Bell Tor and Chinkwell Tor, on the western slope just off the highest point of the ridge path. To come to this group of tors, park at the road below Bonehill Rocks.

SHARPITOR	Lustleigh	771815	262	R ptW

Haytor 4.5 km SSE; Easdon Tor 4 km WNW; Hayne Down lies in front of Haytor; R. Bovey 800 m W and S.

Sharpitor is comprised of large rocks on the footpath from Hammerslake towards Hunters Tor.

SHARPITOR	Walkham	560703	410	R

Sharp Tor [EH]

Leather Tor 400 m SE; Sheepstor 2 km E of S; Leeden Tor 1 km W of N; Black Tor 2 km NE.

A large amount of clitter lies on flat ground to the west and in the same direction a pale-coloured stone, less than a metre high, is inscribed "DPA" one of a series around this tor which is protected by the Dartmoor Preservation Association. Another similar stone stands between this tor and Leather Tor. Access to this pile is straightforward: it's 400 m SE of the higher car park on the B3212 or 500 m S of the lower one, where in summer an ice-cream van is stationed. Near the former parking place is Goatstone Pond, a depression in the ground very close to the road. It has never been known to dry up completely: even in some dry summers, when no water was seen, the peaty mud was still squelchy.

SHAUGH BEACON	Shaugh Prior	547635	263	R

A fairly low pile seen from the north, but the stack slopes steeply to the south. Visible from Beatland Corner, where the road to Cadover Bridge leaves the road to the village after which the height is named. To the west, walkers meet a clear, worn path; this is the "pipe-track" once used for taking material from the china clay pits to the workings above Shaugh Bridge, seen today on the right of the road before the bridge.

SHAVERCOMBE TOR	Plym	594671	350	M

Eastern Tor 1 km NW; Hen Tor 1 km S; R. Plym 500 m NW; Shavercombe Brook to the east, with the waterfall 100 m distant.

Due north is Giant's Basin, a large cairn, behind which stand the most impressive group of stone rows on the moor with the largest standing-stones and three smaller cairns at the north-eastern end of the rows. This tor can be reached from the parking area near Gutter Tor. Walk south along the path to Dittsworthy Warren House, then 1 km E crossing the Plym and negotiating the walls of Hen Tor Farm en route. Walls of an ancient pound are see 100 m below the tor.

SHEARABACK TOR see Shadyback Tor

SHEEPSTOR	Burrator	566682	369	M R

Sheep's Tor [REV. H. BRETON 1911]

Shittistor [SR]

Sharpitor 2 km WNE; Down Tor 2 km NE; Eylesbarrow 3.5 km E; Gutter Tor 2 km SE.

From the east and south of the reservoir, Sheepstor is prominent as the head of a lion or a lion *restant* when approached from the east.

Vian Smith, in *Portrait of Dartmoor*, says that Sheepstor covers 100 acres, which is too incredible to be true. Think of 100 football pitches (flat, of course!) over the tor and you'd cover all the water and most of the forest as well. The rocks do certainly scatter themselves over a wide area, but 100 m square would be nearer the truth. A row of worked stones 1.5 m high maximum climb the hill from the west and descend towards Eylesbarrow. They are inscribed "P.C.W.W." and signify the catchment

area of the reservoir when it was enlarged in 1917. Burrator Lake, as it's sometimes referred to, had a surface area of 116 acres when it was first filled in 1898 and subsequent heightening of the dams enlarged the acreage to 150 by 1928. The tor is the only one which gives its name to the village and parish, which is over 3,400 acres. A steep climb is necessary from whichever direction you take; the easiest to do is from the lane which runs from the east of the church and turns off north-east. Park off the road where the wall ends and climb. Near the summit below the rocks on the northern slope are patches of featherbed, turf and moss which seem harmless but shake when stepped on. Often they hold firm but at other times...

SHELL TOP   Lee Moor   598638   470   R
Penshiel [sr]
Shell Tor [c]
Shiel Top [eh]
Pen Beacon 1 km S; Gt Trowlesworthy Tor 2 km WNW; Gutter Tor 3.5 km NNW; Stalldon 4 km ESE; Broadall lake 800 m E; R. Plym 2.5 km NW.

Superb views over Plymouth and the South Devon Coast, as well as giving a panorama across south-west Dartmoor to the north. Approach Shell Top from Cadover Bridge (GR 555646) and Trowlesworthy Tors. It's uphill most of the way but there again, you have to make some effort to get the result. Anyway, it's all downhill going back, and Cadover Bridge is another haunt of the ice cream seller.

SHELSTONE TOR   W. Okement   558898   400   M
Shellstone [ba]
Shilston [sr]
Sourton Tors 1.5 km W; High Willhays 2.25 km S of E; Black Tor 1 km ESE; W. Okement 300 m NE; Vellake 500 m NW.

One main outcrop and two smaller stacks make up the tor and there is an outlier 50 m away to the north-west. To the west, the ground forms a semi-circle and here hang-gliding groups are often seen. Below, in the Okement Valley, is yet another of the 'Gems' of the moor listed by Crossing, the Island of Rocks. Especially after heavy rain, the water tumbles among the boulders and trees and passes either side of the narrow strip of land. This is also frequented by campers who feel that small though the island be, they are completely surrounded by water. From Meldon car park, follow the route as for Lints Tor, but when the end of the reservoir is passed and you are heading south-east, cross the river by the shed. A steep climb takes you to the tor.

SHILSTONE TOR   Throwleigh   658902   314
Shellstone Tor [SR]
Buttern Tor 2 km SSW; Cosdon Beacon 2.5 km NW; Forder Brook 300 m S.
One of the tors that can hardly be missed from one angle, but from another the walker needs to be within 100 m before he/she realises that a tor is about to loom up. Approaching from the west, the rocks look innocuous, hardly rising above ground level. More people, however, will visit the tor direct from the road which is only 100 m away.
From the old A30 above South Zeal, turn towards Throwleigh and fork right twice, crossing a narrow bridge and a cattle grid. This tor will eventually be seen on the right above the road, 1.5 km south of the bridge.

SHIPLEY TOR   Avon   685632   300   R W
A fine looking middle-sized tor which is at its best when seen from the west bank of the Avon on a level with Black Tor (500 m NW), but it's only legally found by walking from the south.
The reach of the river, above Shipley Bridge and below Brentmoor House (see Black Tor), is yet another site claimed to be a 'gem' by W. Crossing. Man has built up the banks of the Avon to increase the speed and force of the water to wash away silt and lighter material from the tin-bearing rocks. Longatraw, or Long Trough, is such a stretch and can be compared with the Teign above Teign-e-ver bridge below Scorhill Tor (q.v.) and Sandy Hole Pass upstream of the Dart Waterfall, which may be visited on the way to or from Kit Rocks (see Kit Tor). The area is easily gained by leaving the transport at Shipley Bridge, going north along South West Water's private road to the next bridge. Turn south-east to cross the open land through scattered clitter to see the rocks a little to the south, with the wall of the fields of Yelland Farm across your bearing. There is no direct access to the tor. This means that you will have to retrace your steps to get back to your car, so why not visit Black Tor on the journey?

SITTAFORD TOR   Teign   633830   538   R W
Siddaford Tor [C] + [BA] + [EH]
Kes Tor 4.5 km NE; Stannon Tor 2.5 km SSE; Bellever Tor 6 km S; Higher White Tor 5 km SSW; Rough Tor 4.25 km S of SW; North Teign River 600 m NW and N; Lade Hill Stream 1 km SE flowing S.
Although not a very tall pile (a "cliff" of under 2 m all round makes climbing to the summit as easy as walking to Combestone Tor from the road), its altitude gives Sittaford Tor a prominence which is realised from many points in the upper Dart and Teign valleys. Also, it's because it is quite isolated from other outcrops. A stop at the end of the road that runs around Fernworthy Reservoir will leave you a pleasant, but not too demanding, stroll; from GR 659839, take the track through the forest to GR 641844, i.e., roughly north-westerly, to the gate overlooking Teign Head Farm. Turn left and walk with the wood on your left, but drop down slightly to the gap in the wall. Continue on the worn path to the next gate from where Sittaford is uphill to the right. Ahead at the gate are Grey Wethers, the largest double stone circle on the moor, if not in Europe.

SKIR TOR see Scarey Tor

SMALLACOMBE ROCKS   Haytor   755783   c.370   M R
Grea Tor [SR]
Haytor 1.25 km SSE; Saddle Tor 2 km SSW; Holwell Tor 800 m SW; Greator Rocks 800 m NW with Hound Tor behind; Chinkwell Tor 2.5 km W; Becka (or Becky) Brook 500 m W.
Between this tor and Leighon Tor is the parish boundary of Ilsington and Manaton. A line of stones, dressed and inscribed, runs from near the top of Green Lane, Haytor Vale (GR 780774) and can be followed in roughly a north-westerly direction to the Becky Valley. Those to the east of these rocks have names, most of which are connected with the Royal Family of the 1850s. The Duke of Somerset, then resident at Norsworthy Manor, had the stones erected to describe the manor bounds of his land; the date 1854 is found on one face and the previous year's date on another line of stones on Hameldown.
From the lower car park at Haytor, the one with the public conveniences, walk around Haytor itself, leaving it on your left, and go north-westwards for a further kilometre, crossing en route granite railway lines (see Holwell Tor).

SNAPPERS TOR [c]   **Deancombe**   **577693**   **c.300**   **W**

A comparatively large tor but it is assumed that it is not portrayed on OS maps because of its proximity to Down Tor, of which Snappers Tor could be an outer pile or a somewhat detached part of the former. The GRs are necessarily vague as Crossing's guide says that the tor is close to the track from Norsworthy Bridge up the valley to the sites of the farms in Deancombe. However, 300 m is not "close" and a sight of the tor en route to Down Tor will endorse the fact. The main outcrop is obvious when approached from the track near the ruined Middleworth and it is accompanied by big granite rocks. Eastwards is a deep gully, one of many in the area, a relic from the age of the 'tinners', who searched for that ore in the hope that it would make them rich. From Norsworthy Bridge, go south to the stony track 100 m away. Along the track you can find a way uphill to the left, just before Middleworth, tall walls of a house, which have been concreted to prevent erosion or a sudden collapse. Snappers Tor is above and ahead on the horizon. Just above the ruined farm, about 100 m away, is a small pile of rocks, which I've heard (but only once) referred to as Middleworth Tor.

SOURTON TORS   **Sourton**   **543899**   **440**   **M R T**

Shelstone Tor 1.5 km E; Yes Tor nearly 4 km E; Vellake 1 km E; R. Lew 2 km NW.

These tors are the first to be seen when travelling by road from Sourton Cross on the A386 to Tavistock. There seems to be a terrace two-thirds of the way up, on which many craggy piles stand. On the top is another group of outcrops. The rocks are igneous, like granite, but formed on metamorphic slates.The former route from Okehampton to Tavistock ran to the south of the tors and on some OS productions "King Wall" is marked. Most locals call it "King Way" and the track can be quite easily traced from the east of Meldon hamlet to Bearslake, near Lydford, on the A386. Iron Gates was the name of the location where today two small standing stones, 10 m apart, show where the parish boundary of Okehampton was marked by metal gates across the thoroughfare. The "Way" continues south-westerly running collaterally in places with the Rattlebrook Railway under Great Nodden and behind the Dartmoor Inn. Sourton Tors can be reached by walking uphill from the church for 1 km.

SOUTHBEETOR see Longaford Tor

SOUTHCOTT ROCKS see Bowerman's Nose

STANNON TOR   **Postbridge**   **646810**   **450**   **E R**

Birch Tor is behind Water Hill to the east; Hameldon Tor 5.5 km E; Hartland Tor 1.5 km SSW; Higher White Tor 3.75 km SW; Rough Tor 4.75 km WSW; Sittaford Tor 2.5 km NNW; East Dart R. 700 m W; Stannon Brook 300 m E.

Being unkind to this area, the tor is insignificant, just another outcrop, but to the south west of it is the best preserved sheepfold on the moor. A rectangle of high walls, it was used to keep the animals relatively sheltered from the winds and is within easy reach of the farm. In the vicinity and, others have said, in the same four walls, was once a starch factory. As with so many fanciful and even well-intentioned ideas, the production lasted only a few years. It is not on 'Access Land'.

STAPLE TOR, GREAT   **Walkham**   **542760**   **455**   **M R**
Great Roose Tor [DONN 1765]
Steeple Tor [EH]

Roos Tor 600 m N; Gt Mis 2 km NE; Fur Tor 8.5 km NNE; N. Hessary Tor 4 km ESE; Vixen Tor 1.75 km S; Mid Staple Tor lies to the SW and is passed if the route to the tor suggested below is taken; R. Walkham 1 km W; Beckamoor Brook 800 m W and S.

One of the moor's spectacular sites, Gt Staple ranks in my eyes with Gt Mis, Gt Links, Fur and Beardown Tors as fine examples of what the forces of nature can do with a million years. Two tall stacks dominate the scene standing on the highest point of the hill with 40 m of cropped grass between them. Other solid piles add to the overall spectacle and a 360° sweep all over the moor makes this venue a must for explorers. To the south-east, roughly halfway to Merrivale are remains of granite sett-makers' bankers, or benches. The men often knelt with their knees under the ledge to shape, smooth and flatten pieces of rock for a particular purpose and as proof, there

are small heaps of granite on either side of the bench. This was set up by standing upright two thin slabs about 60 cm apart with a capstone laid across which acted as the surface on which to work. The men faced uphill so as to lessen the pressure on their backs. Access to Staple Tor is simply explained and does not take too long. From a small car park on the north of the B3357 under little Staple Tor (on the top of the rise from Merrivale going towards Tavistock where the road flattens out), walk 1 km NNE via both Little and Mid Staple Tors to their larger companion.

STAPLE TOR, LITTLE   Walkham   539753   380
Vixen Tor 1 km SSE; Feather Tor 1 km SSW with Pew Tor behind it; Mid Staple Tor 300 m NNE: The tor is 250 m from the road.

STAPLE TOR, MID   Walkham   540756   431
Gt Staple Tor 400 m NNE; King's Tor 2.5 km SE; Feather and Pew Tors SSW; Vixen Tor 1.5 km S; Cox Tor 1 km NW.

Three main piles but forming one raised mound with much clitter to the south and west. A wall of over 2 m faces east, south and west. See Great Staple Tor for directions.

STEEPERTON TOR   Taw   618888   532   H M P R

Yes Tor 4 km WNW; Oke Tor 1.5 km NNW; Belstone Tor 3 km W of N; Hound Tor 1 km ENE; Wild Tor 1.25 km SSE; Gt Links Tor 7 km WSW; R. Taw 400 m W; Steeperton Brook 400 m SE to NE.
Steep it definitely is: from all sides except the south a slope of 45° is negotiated for most of the way and the gradient varies in such a way that like several ascents on Dartmoor you think you are at the summit when a further climb confronts you. Once at the top of the hill, a line of stacks of uniform height stretch from north to south for 200 m. The tor seems most impressive seen from Taw Marsh on the way back from Belstone across the flat valley floor. Due west, the line of a wall can be seen going away from Steeperton, having made its way up the side of the Taw before angling right. Locally known as the Long North Wall, it meets and forms a side of Sammy Arnold's Lane, the track marked on the map running almost east-west towards High Willhays. Just to the north of the wall's angle a track meets the Taw and crosses Knock Mine Ford. Above the crossing place is Knock Mine itself. Approach from Belstone Moorgate and follow the stony track past Winter Tor and Oke Tor, with Knattborough Tor between them, descending to cross the Taw at the ford. Carry on for another hundred metres or so and turn left so that you can steadily climb up to the tor from the south-west. It is longer, but easier.

STENGA TOR   W. Okement   568880   532   K

Le West Soll [RISDON]
Steincator [SR]
Steingetorr [SR]
Stinka Tor [C]
Westsolle [B]

Black Tor 1 km N; High Willhays 2 km NE; Dinger Tor 1.75 km E; Lints Tor 1.25 km ESE; Kitty Tor 600 m S; W. Okement 500 m E and N.
Surrounded by marsh in all but very dry seasons; silhouette of a resting camel when viewed from the south-east when the tor is on the skyline.
From Sourton Church, walk towards the Tors above you, but bear left when the wall turns. Go towards the grassy mounds on the near horizon; once past them ascend Corn Ridge to Branscombe's Loaf. Keep on the same contour, south-east for 1.5 km to the tor.

STONESLADE TOR [EH]   Widecombe   708781   c.400   R

Corndon Tor 4.5 km SW; Bellever Tor 6.5 km WSW; Chinkwell Tor 2 km E; Haytor 5 km ESE:
Situated about 1 km S of Hameldon Beacon, from the north the tor is seen as only a low rock, but from the opposite direction it is found to be a 2–3 m high wall facing south and 20 m across.
On the Two Moors Way, the tor is best approached from Widecombe, up Church Way onto the southern end of the ridge, then follow the wall as it turns right or north. The tor is below the horizon 1 km away.

STONETOR HILL   Teign   649856   410   K W

Stone Tor [C]

Kes Tor 1.75 km ENE; Sittaford Tor 3 km SSW; Watern Tor 2.5 km NW; Hound Tor 4 km NNW.
A very small outcrop which at first glance seems to have been built into the wall of the enclosures of Teignhead Farm. The rocks are only 3 m high at most and can easily be missed, unless you are on the perambulation walk, in which case you might just conceivably look at the tor on the way to the Longstone. From Batworthy (GR 662865), go 1.5 km SW. The tor is 600 m from the edge of Fernworthy Forest along the same wall. There may be patches of marshy ground if a direct route is taken.

STRANE TOR [C]   Princetown   c.612718   c.360

"A small pile," says our William; so small, in fact, that the name "Tor" is hardly applicable. There are two possibilities in the area which can covet the title: one is a scattering of medium-sized boulders found on the east bank of the Strane. None of them could in any way be described as a tor, outcrop or pile. These are seen to the north-east of the footpath from Whiteworks 100 m from it. The slightly more probable Strane Tor is further upstream, roughly 300 m from the rocks and nearer the water. A small cliff-like formation, barely 2 m high, with grass on top amid other larger rocks, similar to Flat Tor but smaller, is seen from the west bank north-east of the big boulder on the opposite bank. It can be approached from the footpath which goes north-east from Peat Cot (waymarked) and where the path turns north to follow the wall, keep ahead to drop down the Strane. The "tor" is in front of you, but you have to look carefully and not blink.

SWELL TOR	**Walkham**	**560733**	**400**	**Q R**

North Hessary Tor 2 km ENE; Ingra Tor 1.25 km SSW; Walkham Valley W; Yes Tor Brook S.
There is no tor on the summit of the hill today, but it is highly likely that before quarrying was begun, some form of rocky outcrop could be seen in the vicinity. One small pile of rock exists, 200 m S of the main quarry site, overlooking Yes Tor Brook. Allowing that all walkers in this area are aware of the dangers that befall even the most careful of people, a visit to the site of what was probably Swell Tor can be made by following the Princetown railway from the town until it begins to swing north. Cut across the turf, making a gradual ascent north-westwards, but pay attention on nearing the top as you will find you are suddenly faced with a hole in front of you! It's quite a drop, so it will be best to turn south to the outcrop.

TAVY CLEAVE SHARP see Sharp Tor, Tavy

TAVY CLEAVE TORS	**Tavy**	**554832**	**424**	

The five tors in the group are each spectacularly perched over Tavy Cleave. Sharp Tor is the principle stack and the others form equally impressive silhouettes from the west, or from the valley bottom. Arrive at these rocks as for Sharp Tor (q.v.).

THORNWORTHY TOR	**Teign**	**664851**	**424**	**R**

Kes Tor 1 km N; Middle Tor 800 m NE; Shapley Tor 4.5 km SE.
Enclosed but accessible by stiles which have been placed at intervals over the wall. Fernworthy Forest, 1 km W, was established in 1919 to restore timber after the 1914–1918 war, and to enhance the appearance of the reservoir which was planned. It was completed in 1936. Come to the tor by way of Frenchbeer Rock (q.v.) then aim WSW while avoiding any marshy patches on the way.

THREE BARROWS	**Erme**	**653626**	**461**	**R T**

Three Barrows Hill [JC]
Three Barrows Tor [RW] + [B]
Three Burrows [EH]
Western Whittaburrow 3 km N; Eastern Whittaburrow 3 km NNE; Sharp Tor (Wacka) 1 km SE; Sharp Tor (Erme) 1 Km SSW; Stalldon 1.75 km S of W; R. Erme W; Red Brook NE running E; Glaze Brook SE.
The cairns (they are all entirely of stones now) stand on the watershed between two large catchment areas, the R. Erme and the R. Avon, and its position suggests that a rocky formation should be found, but what is there is covered by burial mounds.
To the immediate west runs Redlake railway, designed by R. Hansford Worth and built in 1910. It is 12 km from Redlake to Bittaford past Leftlake works, 1 km NNW from the top of the hill. The clay workings were in operation from 1922 to 1932, leaving behind large heaps of spoil and a lake. The tor is reached via Sharp Tor (Erme) (q.v.).

TOP TOR	**Widecombe**	**736762**	**432**	**M R**

Four piles are spaced almost equally apart on the hill: three rocky ones and one heap of stones, which is the highest. Rippon Tor 1.25 km SE; Pil Tor 300 m SSW. Hameldown rises the other side of the East Webburn, which is 2 km W.
The road from Bovey Tracey to Widecombe at Hemsworthy Gate is 300 m away, so you can leave the car, bike or camel here and stroll uphill to the tor.

TOR ROCKS	**Ivybridge**	**641591**	**230**	**Q**

Hangershell Rock 1.25 km N or W. Other tors are not in sight from here, but that is hardly surprising because only Tristis Rock, 1 km W of N (Hall Tor) has the word as part of its name and, even then, it is the lesser-known appellation. The village of Harford, passed on the way to the moorgate, is another 'Gem'. R. Erme 1 km W; Butterbrook 100 m N.

An easy walk to Tor Rocks is had from the moorgate: follow the wall south to Butterbrook, cross it then head west for just over 200 m.

TOR ROYAL see Hessary Tor, South

TORRYCOMBE TOR see Whitehill Tor

TORS END	Belstone	614927	400	R

The most northerly outcrop of the Belstone range of tors. See also Belstone Tors and Higher Tor.

TRISTIS ROCK	Ivybridge	638600	c.250	R

Hall Tor [c]

Butterdon Hill 2.25 km SE; Sharp Tor 2 km NE; Stalldon 2 km N.
A single "Lump" of rocks best seen from the north when it stands out on the skyline.

TROWLESWORTHY TOR, GT	Plym	580643	357	Q R

Hen Tor 2 km NE; Pen Beacon 2.5 km SE; Shell Top 2 km S of E; Legis Tor 1.5 km NNW; R. Plym N-NW-W; Spanish Lake E and NE.

One large tor with varying craggy heights and caves, this tor has rocks of a slightly pinkish hue and was quarried as an alternative to the more usual grey granite. The rock is elongated north-west to south-east. It overlooks the china-clay complex to the south, but it is to the east and north that the greens, browns and greys of the moor are preferable.

Trowlesworthy Warren was one of several on the banks of the Plym serving numerous teams of tin-streamers; they were unaware that in their future, someone would draw longitude 4°W through

the tor. Between this outcrop and its lower namesake, is a granite cylinder seemingly left behind; it has been suggested that it was a flagpole base for Devonport Dockyard which became obsolete as the buyer changed his or her mind, or a plinth for a statue that was of a controversial nature as the hero who may have been carved in perpetuity, complained because he wasn't dead yet. Whatever the reason and cause, it's a good talking point. After Little Trowlesworthy, continue south-east, passing the cylinder on the way to Great Trowlesworthy.

TROWLESWORTHY TOR, LT	Plym	578645	330	Q R

Gt Trowlesworthy Tor 300 m SE; Legis Tor 1.5 km NW; Gutter Tor 2.5 km N; Hen Tor 2 km NE; Shadyback Tor, not marked on the OS maps, is 1.5 km WNW; R. Plym NW; Spanish Lake E and NE.
Like its companion, this tor is almost on an axis, this time roughly north-south. A bank of rubble

extends to the north-west, clear signs that quarries were worked here also. On the far bank of Spanish Lake is yet another former warren, Willings Walls. Like all the land on this side of the Plym, Little T stands on National Trust property, a fact gleened by looking for the NT sign on the way from Cadover Bridge. Go east along the track which leads off the former road to Cornwood, cross the Blackabrook near the sign, pass the Warren House on its west side then head east, uphill to the tor.

TUNHILL ROCKS   Widecombe   731758   390   M
A scattering of boulders and stones on the slope below Pil Tor, to the west of that group. A few trees grow among them, holly included. Nothing much in that, perhaps, but there's nothing of any note in this site, either.

UGBOROUGH BEACON   Bittaford   668591   378   R
Beacon Rocks
Eastern Beacon
East Pigedon Tor [c]
Western Beacon 2km SW; Butterdon Hill 1.25km S of W; Three Barrows 3.5km NNW.
Two main groups of rock piles; large white pole to the south.

ULLESTOR see Roborough Rock

VIXEN TOR   Walkham   542742   312   N R
Great Staple Tor 2 km N; Great Mis Tor 3.25 km NE; Kings Tor 1.25 km SE; Pew Tor 1.25 km SW behind Heckwood Tor; Feather Tor 700 m W; R. Walkham E; Beckamoor Brook W.
The tallest, not the highest, tor on the moor at 30 m, so everyone is told. I wonder at this figure and would state that Luckey Tor runs Vixen very close. Very few choices can be made if you need to climb to the top, but some rock basins can be looked at if you think it's worth the effort. Easy to

reach: from Pork Hill, walk south-east, but avoid the springs of the Beckamoor by keeping to the left, then aim for the unmistakable pile using the stile over the west-facing wall. For many years visiting has been denied, but more than one agency is determining a way of reclaiming access to this fascinating tor.

VURTORRE see Fur Tor

WACKA TOR [EH]   South Brent   663621   407   M R
Sharp Tor [c]
From the highest stack: Chinkwell Tor on the horizon NNE; Black Tor 2 km NE; Shipley Tor against the hillside just to the right of Black Tor 2.5 km away; Ugborough Beacon 3 km S; Butterdon Hill 3.5 km SSW; Sharp Tor (Erme) 1.5 km WSW; Three Barrows 1 km NW; Red Brook N; East Glaze Brook 500 m S and E; Avon 2 km E.

A scattering of six or seven outcrops, none of which exceed 4 m high crown the hill. From the south, the most westerly stack does have a "sharp" outline. The most complicated series of stone rows on the moor are found 1 km S of the most easterly rocks: some experts say that there are two triple rows and a double; some, three triples and a single; others, four doubles. They are a few metres from the wall between East and West Glaze Brook. Wacka Tor can be reached from Harford Moorgate. Walk north-east to the top of Piles Hill (a steady ascent) then continue in the same direction for another 1.5 km, crossing the West Glaze halfway towards the tor.

WAIN TOR see Mis Tor, Little

WAS TOR   Lydford   500829   +240   E R
Hare Tor 5 km ENE; Brentor 4 km SW; R. Burn S and E; R. Lyd 600 m W.
Not a very tall rock but craggy and of basalt, not granite. It rises above the track of the former railway links between Plymouth and Okehampton and Plymouth and Launceston.
Stop before you reach the southern car park for Lydford Gorge and go along the track immediately west of the railway bridge towards Wastor Farm. Turn right in 200 m then left on the footpath. Was (pronounced to rhyme with 'gas') Tor is behind barbed wire, on **private land**, on the right in another 200 m.

WATERN TOR   Wallabrook   629868   526   K M R
Thurlesdon [B] + [RISDON]
Waterdontorr [SR]
Wild Tor 1 km NNW; Kes Tor 3.75 km S of E; Hangingstone Hill 1.25 km SW; Yes Tor and High Willhays about 6 km NW; North Teign 1.25 km SE; Wallabrook 200 m W, in Watern Combe.
The lamellar bedding seen on some rocky outcrops is shown here in abundance. Each pile, in an almost north-south line, has this formation and it is probably because of this that the "Thurlestone", or holed stone, has been eroded between the most northerly stacks. Visit Watern Tor by way of Wild Tor (q.v.) then head across the stream to the tor roughly the same bearing. A longer route can be followed from Batworthy from where you walk along the edge of the forest westwards to drop down to Teignhead Clapper, the bridge with slabs of granite (GR 639844), and thence up the stream NW to meet and trace a banked wall NNW for 2.5 km, reaching the tor via the cairn on the ridge, south of your objective.

WAYDOWN TOR see White Tor, Lower

WELSTOR ROCK   Buckland   736730   c.380   R
Buckland Beacon 200 m WNW; Rippon Tor 3 km NNE.
One small compact stack, which can be approached from Cold East Cross. Go SSE to meet a wall on your left near which is a boundary stone showing the border between Ashburton and Buckland parishes. Keep the wall on the left and in 700 m, opposite Buckland Beacon, turn left through the gate to the rock.

WEST MIL see Mill Tor, West

WESTERN BEACON   Ivybridge   654575   332   Q R
Eastern Beacon to the north-east, Pen Beacon to the north-west, in the distance. Five cairns stand on the hill, and people have been moving stone ever since. One of the quarries here supplied stone for the viaducts which take the railway above Ivybridge and Cornwood and workings have covered the former crown of the rocks which stood on the summit. There is a small outcrop just below the top quarry, 50 m S of the summit, 400 m on the southern end of a long line of boundary stones forming the edge of Harford and Ugborough parishes. (Harford is now part of the parish of Ivybridge, although its own church is worth a visit en route to the moorgate.)

WESTSOLLE see Stenga Tor

WHITE TOR   Peter Tavy   542787   468   M P R
Whit Tor [EH] + [BG]
The Peter Stone, in early 19th century accounts, sits on Peter Tor, a name for this tor now not used.

Beardown Tor 6 km ESE; Great Mis Tor 2.5 km SE; Great Staple Tor 3 km S; Lynch Tor 3 km NE; Boulters Tor 2 km WSW; Brentor 7 km WNW; Collybrook 1 km S; Youlden Brook 1.5 km N; R. Tavy 2 km W.

White Tor comprises a scattering of outcrops over a distance of 400 m on a W-E line, and is mainly of non-granite trap rock.

To the east is another tall standing stone, Longstone on some maps, "Lanson" in local talk. Several ruined cairns give the appearance that the tor is one single mixture of stones and outcrops. The place can be seen at close quarters by beginning your walk at Wapsworthy (Farm) just south of which is a footpath; go between the two walls and when it opens out onto the common, aim for the rocks 1 km further on. Avoid the springs en route.

WHITE TOR, HIGHER   W. Dart   620786   527   R
Higher Whiten Tor [EH]
Whitten Tor [C] + [SR]

Donn's map shows this as Waydown Tor, which is incorrect. It is Lower White Tor which lies 700 m N; Bellever Tor 3.25 km SE; Beardown Tor 2 km SW; North Hessary Tor 6 km SW; Gt Mis Tor 6 km WSW; Devil's Tor 2.5 km WNW; Fur Tor 5.5 km NW; Longaford Tor 750 m SW; which will be visited if walking the ridge from Crockern Tor before reaching this outcrop; Cherrybrook 700 m E; E. Dart 1 km W.

A small cairn tops the summit of this tor; it is not particularly spectacular but a wide view of the inner regions of the moor as well as many landmarks is had. From Crockern Tor (q.v.) 3 km away, the approach is from the south; or if from Two Bridges you keep to the banks of the R. Dart past Wistman's Wood, turn uphill at the next wall before the river is met.

WHITE TOR, LOWER   W. Dart   619792   507   R
Waydown Tor [SR]

Sittaford Tor 4 km NNE; Broad Down 2 km NE; Birch Tor 6 km ENE; Rough Tor 1.5 km WNW; Flat Tor 2.5 km NNW; Cherrybrook (in Hollowcombe Bottom) 400 m E; W Dart 600 m W.

Again the more modern version of maps are at odds with Donn's cartographical skills as these rocks are, on his map, named as Bearyonder Tor. Due north of its bigger namesake, access to this tor is also from either of the routes described above.

WHITEHILL TOR   Lee Moor   575614   c.170   R
Torrycombe Tor [C, AS ALTERNATIVE] + [EH]

Crownhill Tor 500 m S; Blackalder Tor 700 m WNW, to the right of the booster mast, among the trees. The rocks are perched on a very steep slope to the east where the Torrycombe Brook flows from E to S. The less steep gradients are to the south and west and, being so close to the road from Cornwood to Shaugh Prior (100 m off to the south), directions are not needed. Quarried rocks and remains of spoil tips lie around especially to the south and west and a large outcrop is 100 m S before there too, the ground steepens.

WHITESTONE see Heltor Rocks

WHITTEN TOR (HIGHER) see White Tor, Higher

WHITTENKNOWLES ROCKS   Plym   585670   330

Simply a small rock-pile among other scattered boulders, but they stand among a group of hut-circles, enclosures and banks above Scout Hut, which is 500 m to the west.

WILD TOR   Wallabrook   622876   531   nr K M R

Watern Tor 1 km SSE; Steeperton Tor 1.25 km NNW; High Willhays and Yes Tor 5 km NW; Hound Tor 1.5 km NNE; Rival Tor 2 km ENE; Wallabrook 600 m E; Steeperton Brook 600 m W and N.

Large blocks make up the outcrops of this tor and is one which attracts many groups of youngsters probably because there are so many other tors to visit in this area. Many of them miss the granite kiln to the south of the rocks on the ridge. It is a cube, now partly collapsed, just over a metre in each direction, and is known as a meiler. To have a look at Wild (pronounced 'Willed') Tor, come from Steeperton Tor or, from the ford SW of Steeperton, go 1 km SE.

WILLINGSTONE ROCK   **Moreton**   **756887**   **323**   **N X**
Willistone [J]
Less than 3 km N of Moreton, not NW as [J] says.

WIND TOR   **Widecombe**   **706758**   **375**   **M R**
Corndon Tor 2.5 km SW; Sharp Tor 3.5 km SSW; Rowden Tor 1 km WNW.
Lying between the two Wallabrooks at the most southerly end of Hameldown, the tor consists of 2 m-high cliffs with grassy summit, covering a few score metres. From Widecombe, go uphill past Southcombe on the left and on the top of the hill walk south for 500 m.

WINTER TOR   **Belstone**   **610915**   **c.420**   **R**
Higher Tor 300 m ENE; Oke Tor 1.5 km S; Knattborough 600 m S; Yes Tor 3 km SW; West Mill Tor 2.25 km WSW; East Okement 300 m W.
One almost conical pile, with mostly clitter, as you would expect, falling away to the west. From Belstone Moorgate, walk along the track going south for 2 km. Winter Tor is 30 m off the track to the right.

WOODER GOYLE ROCKS   **Widecombe**   **716778**   **c.370**
Consisting of large boulders on the slope of Wooder Goyle itself, a deep defile on the slopes of Hameldown Beacon. They are a few metres above enclosure walls, but to explore them needs care and patience.

YAR TOR   **Dart**   **679740**   **410**   **R**
Sharp Tor 1 km SSE; Laughter Tor 3 km NW; Corndon Tor 1 km E; E. Dart 800 m W.

Although not an outstanding tor to look at, like several others, the climbing becomes worthwhile as you ascend because the extent of the panorama is unsurpassed – equalled yes, but none better. From the top of Dartmeet Hill on the Ashburton–Two Bridges road, walk 700 m N. Or start at the privately owned car park at Dartmeet (called Badgers' Holt), and go ENE till you can go up no further.

YELVERTON ROCK see Roborough Rock

YES TOR   W. Okement   581901   **619 H K M P R T**
Ernestorre [B]
Grenestor [RISDON]

Gt Links Tor 4.5 km SW; Cosdon Beacon 5.5 km ENE; Belstone Tor 3.75 km NE; West Mill Tor 1 km NNE; East Mill Tor 2 km S of E; Fur Tor 6.5 km S; Redaven Brook 500 m E and N; W. Okement 2 km SW; Snipe's Gully 1.25 km NW.

The highest by far of all the tors, and one of the most famous because of its name, Yes Tor has wide views over much of west and north Devon as well as Dartmoor. One km to the south lies the only point higher, High Willhays, and as there is only a drop of 7 m between them, the ridge is referred to as "the roof of Devon". The seven-yearly beating of the Okehampton parish boundary (the moorland part), avoids the ascent to the top, following the line of fine stones from Sandy Ford (GR 574879) to Middle Ford (GR 598912) in a NNW direction, but the perambulators of 1240 saw this elevated point as an obvious edge to Henry III's Forest.

Extensive clitter lies on three sides and so care should be taken if you approach the summit from any direction other than this: from the "ring-road" at New Bridge, walk west for 1.5 km to meet a rough track. Keep on this track bearing north when it branches near the top of the ridge. Yes Tor is in fact visible for all of the way (look for the flagpole and trig. point).

YSFOTHER see Hessary Tor, North

ZEAL TOR [EH]   Avon   673639   382

Unfortunately there is no tor on the summit of Zeal Hill: two small and inconspicuous boulders can easily be missed! So why the "Zeal Tor Tramway"? I believe that the name was derived from the Celtic 'tor(r)' which meant 'a wood' and that the presence of woods in the valleys of the Avon, Bala Brook and Middle Brook, far more extensive than today's scattering of trees, was the basis of the railway's name. The latter can be quite easily traced from above Shipley Bridge, where it had its terminus, north-easterly to Redlake. It was in operation only from 1846 to 1850, but some interesting relics are found: stones showing distances from the workings include one inscribed 3/4 (GR 658649). The remains of the associated naphtha works and settling pits are overlooking the car park at Shipley Bridge – Uncle Ab's House at Middle Brook Head (GR 656 639) was the stabling quarters for the change of horses necessary during their journey. Ab himself was said to have been forever intoxicated and, like his former abode today, the worst for wear.